Bass Guitar Scale Manual.

We are the music-makers,
    And we are the dreamers of dreams,
Wandering by lone sea breakers,
    And sitting by desolate streams;
World-losers and world-forsakers,
    On whom the pale moon gleams;
Yet we are the movers and shakers
    Of the world forever, it seems.

A. W. E. O'Shaughnessy, *Ode,* stanza 1

Bass Guitar Scale Manual.

Amsco Publications
New York/London/Sydney

Photographs:

page 67	*Rick Danko*	Gary Legon
page 107	*John Entwhistle*	courtesy Track Records
page 119	*Chris Squier*	courtesy Atlantic Record
page 129	*Kenny Passarelli*	Herb Wise
page 140	*Lee Vinson*	

Cover and poster designed by Pearce Marchbank Studio
Book designed by Carol Zimmerman

Order No. AM 14796
US International Standard Book Number: 0.8256.4064.4
UK International Standard Book Number: 0.7119.0587.8
Library of Congress Catalog Card Number: 74-21599

Exclusive Distributors:
Music Sales Corporation
257 Park Avenue South, New York, NY 10010, USA
Music Sales Limited
8/9 Frith Street, London W1V 5TZ England
Music Sales Pty. Limited
120 Rothschild Street, Rosebery, Sydney, NSW 2018, Australia

Printed in the United States of America by
Vicks Lithograph and Printing Corporation

CONTENTS

INTRODUCTION

The study of scales should be integrated into your daily practice. Do not limit yourself, however, to only playing scales. They are supposed to supplement your studies, not be the whole of them. Also, don't start off practicing the scales two hours each day. Ten or fifteen minutes to warm up your hands will be adequate for some time.

When you begin practicing a scale, play it first a few times slowly and vigorously. Later, after you loosen up, play it quicker and lighter.

SYSTEMS ANALYSIS

The electric bass has four strings, and the tablature system used in this book (based on a combination of the Spanish and French tablature systems) uses four lines:

Vertical lines (called bar lines) divide the staff into measures:

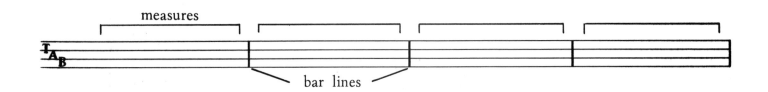

Each of the four lines of the tablature staff represents a bass string: the top line stands for the highest sounding string (G string), the next line stands for the next string down (D string), the next-to-bottom line stands for the A string, and the bottom line stands for the lowest sounding string (E string).

TABLATURE

top line (highest sounding string)

BASS STRINGS

bottom line (lowest sounding string)

An *o* on the tablature staff indicates that you play a specific string open or unfingered. For example, an *o* on the bottom line means that you play the lowest sounding string open.

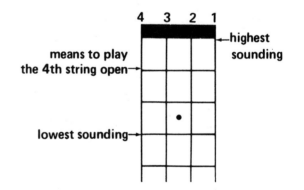

means to play
the 4th string open→

lowest sounding→

←highest
sounding

An *o* on the 3rd line indicates that you play the 3rd string open.

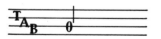

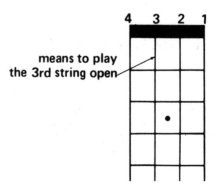

means to play
the 3rd string open

An Arabic number on the tablature staff indicates the specific string and fret position to play. A *5* on the bottom line indicates that you play the lowest sounding string fretted on the 5th fret. Left hand fingering appears immediately below the tab notes:

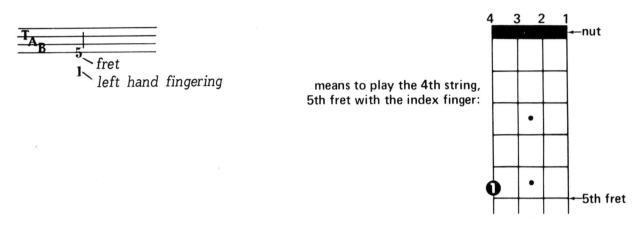

means to play the 4th string, 5th fret with the index finger:

A *7* on the next line up indicates that you play the 3rd string fretted at the 7th fret.

Left hand fingering is indicated *1, 2, 3, and 4* representing the index, middle, ring, and pinky of the fretting hand. Right hand fingering is notated *i* and *m* (index and middle) or ⊓ and V (pick downstroke and pick upstroke).

RIGHT HAND FINGERING

Bass players who pluck the strings with the index and middle fingers of the right hand (*i* and *m*) should alternate the starting fingers. The two possibilities are starting with the middle finger and following with the index finger (*m i m i m i m i*) or starting with the index finger and following with the middle finger (*i m i m i m i m*). This will lead to right hand independence.

Bass players who play with a pick should also alternate. The two possibilities here are starting with a pick downstroke and then an upstroke (⊓ v ⊓ v ⊓ v ⊓ v) or starting with a pick upstroke and then a downstroke (v ⊓ v ⊓ v ⊓ v ⊓).

Anton Rubinstein, a famous nineteenth century pianist and composer, once remarked, "Scales should never sound dry. If you are not interested in them, work with them until you do become interested in them."

8

SCALES IN OPEN POSITION

Open position scales are scales using open or unfingered strings. The open position scales are intended for the beginning student but can be played profitably by advanced students as well. Allow a few days practice on each scale before taking up the next one. Before you introduce a new scale into your daily practice, play the ones you've already learned.

The A Scales

A MAJOR SCALE

The A major scale is an important open string scale starting with the 3rd* string open or unfingered.

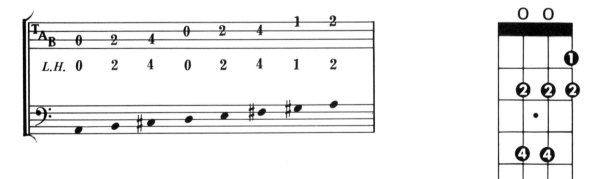

Many songs are written in the key of A because of the sonority provided by the open A string both in the bass (3rd string) and in the guitar (5th string).

*Bass strings are numbered from 1 to 4 starting with the highest sounding string (1st string) and going to the lowest sounding string (4th string).

In the following exercise, observe that the right hand starts and ends the scale with the same finger or pick stroke—both the first and last notes in the exercise are played by the index finger (or pick downstroke). If the first note (the note A) is played by the index finger and the last note (again A), by the middle finger, you failed to alternate somewhere in between. *The alternation must be strict*, otherwise you'll be learning habits that will be difficult to correct later.

EXERCISE

A 6th SCALE

A scale closely related to the A major scale is the A 6th scale.

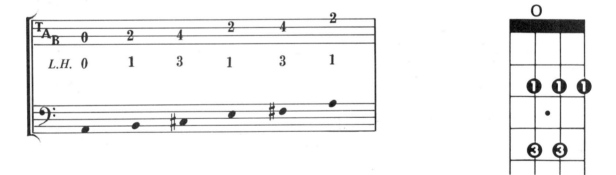

This five note scale (called a *pentatonic scale*) is considered the prototype of all scales because of its ancient origin. It can be easily played on the piano by playing the black keys only (F# 6th scale).

EXERCISE

10

This scale is frequently used in improvisation, particulary in *soul* tunes. It nicely supports an A major or A6 chord as in this example.

PROGRESSION #1

A 7TH SCALE

The A 7th scale is also used in improvisation. It is widely used in rock and blues tunes.

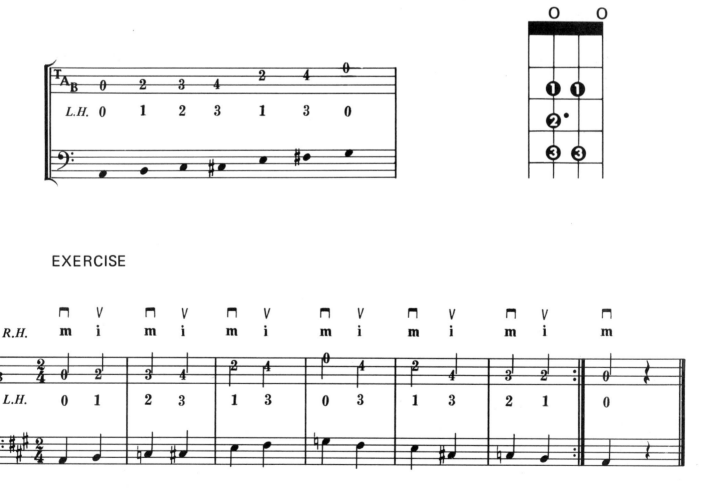

EXERCISE

Playable with A7 and A9 chords, extra punch is provided by the open 3rd string.

PROGRESSION #2

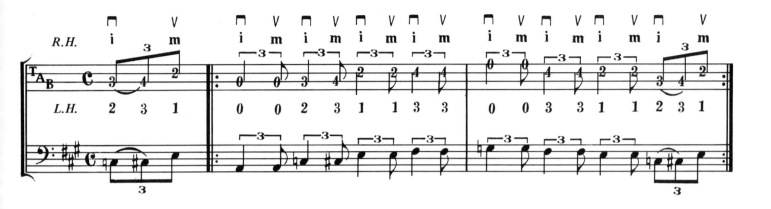

A BLUES SCALE

Related to the A 7th scale is the A blues scale—a favorite of hard rock bands.

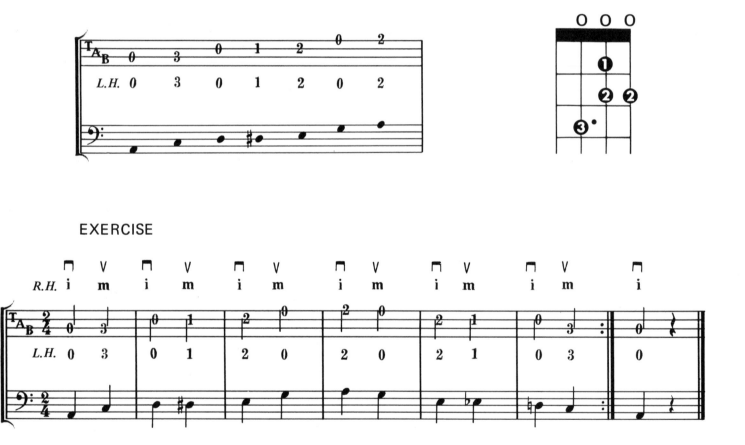

EXERCISE

This scale is minor and can be successfully played under any A minor chord. In general, the quality of the blues scale is such that it is often employed with dominant 7th chords as well (A7, C7, G7, etc.), sometimes doubling the lead guitar which characteristically uses this type of scale in rock and blues improvisation.

PROGRESSION #3

A NATURAL MINOR SCALE

The natural minor is the fundamental minor scale from which all the other minor scales are derived (the blues scale is actually a hybrid).

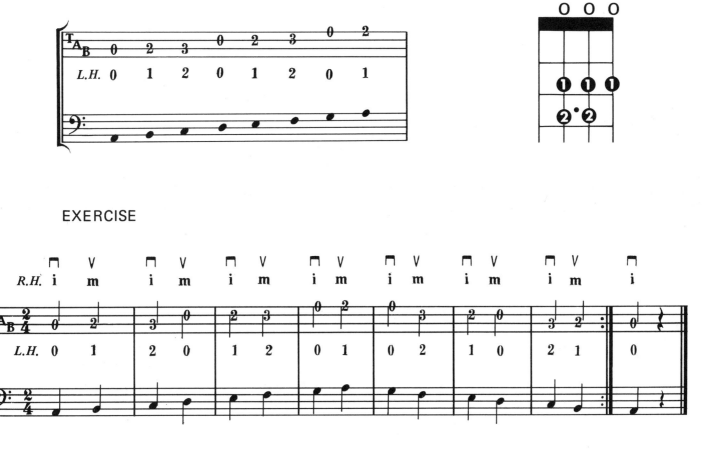

EXERCISE

Not that often used as a bass line, the scale has its moments—as in this, from *House of the Rising Sun*.

PROGRESSION #4

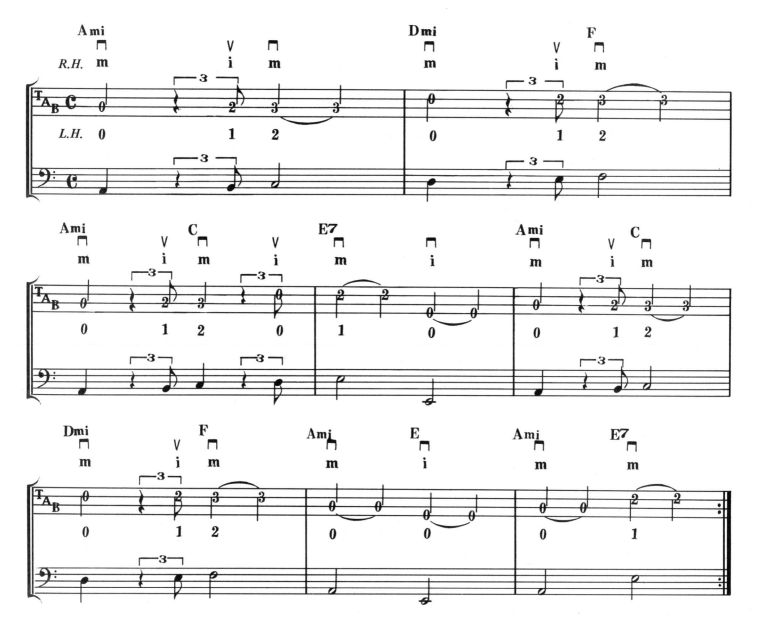

The A minor jazz and the A natural minor scales are similar. The difference is in the 6th degree or step (the 6th note from the left is the 6th degree of the scale). The natural minor is the unaltered minor scale. The jazz scale is said to have a raised 6th. Compare the two:

A MINOR JAZZ SCALE

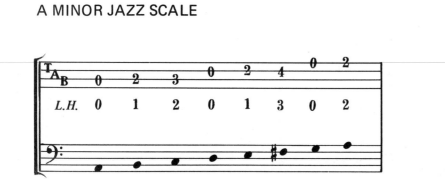
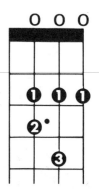

This scale has a distinctly minor sound and is used for improvising with any A minor chord (Ami6, Ami7, Ami9, etc.). It conveys a laid-back feeling typical of softer, melodic tunes.

EXERCISE

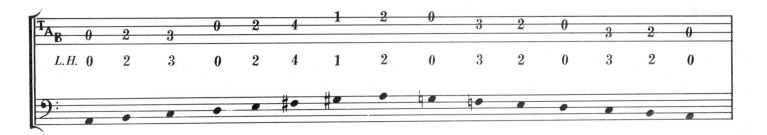

A MELODIC MINOR SCALE

This completes all the popular A minor scales in use. It is the only scale where the descending form differs from the ascending form. Descending it is identical to the A natural minor. Ascending the first five notes are the same as in the A natural minor with notes six and seven like those found in the A major scale.

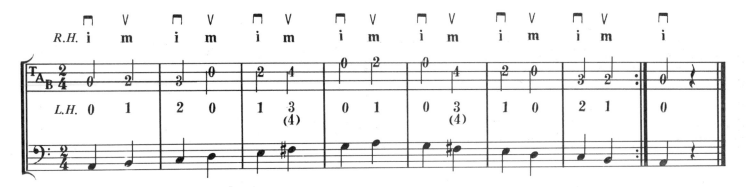

The exercise provides a good workout because of the change in fingering on the descending side.

EXERCISE

The E Scales

E MAJOR SCALE

A good reason for learning this scale is that more blues songs have been written in the key of E major than any other key.

One explanation for the popularity of this key is that the lowest pitched string on both the bass and guitar is the tonic.

EXERCISE

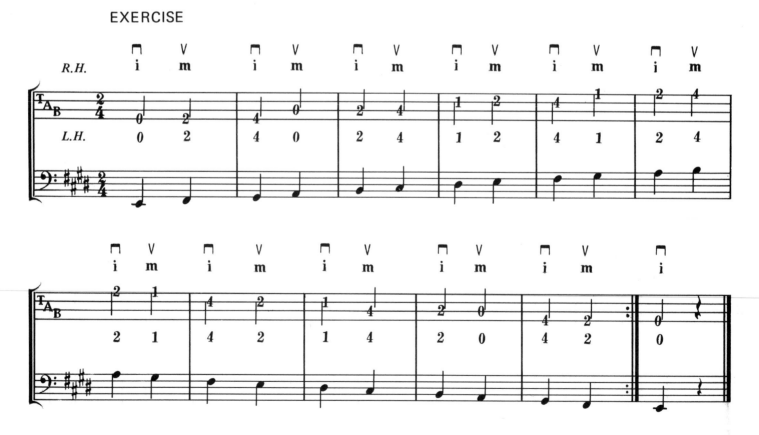

Take the next line at an up-tempo.

PROGRESSION #5

E 6TH SCALE

Move the A 6th scale pattern over one string and start it on the 4th string, and you have the E 6th scale.

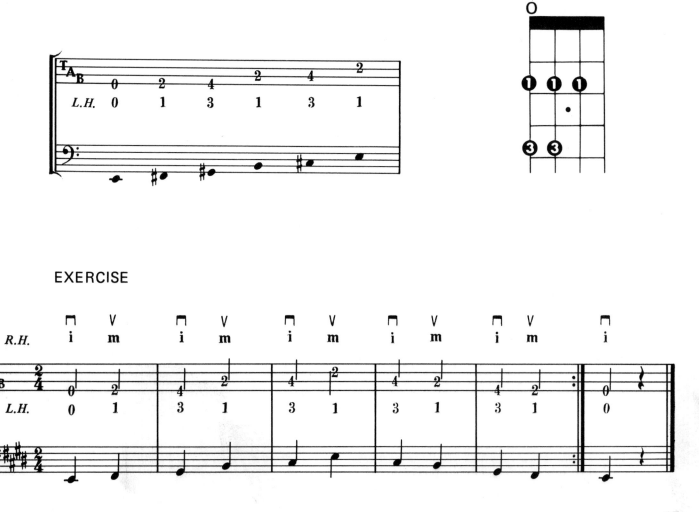

EXERCISE

This scale is often used to fill out a line beneath an E major or E6 chord. Combine the E 6th scale and the A 6th scale in the same progression. Notice how they join together to form a familiar musical idea.

PROGRESSION #6

E 7TH SCALE

The E 7th scale is easy to play and equally as useful in a hard driving rock tune as in a slow, meandering blues.

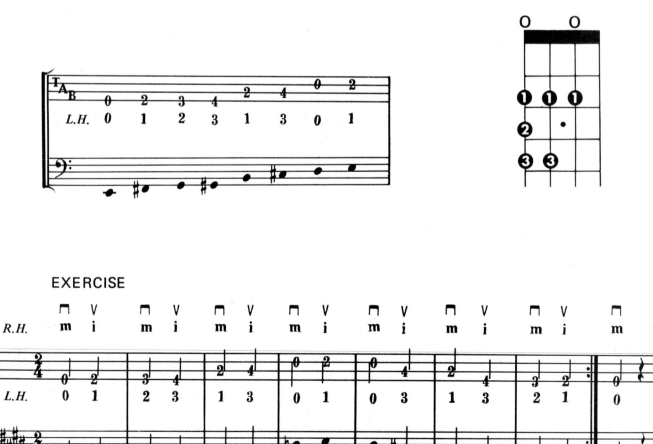

EXERCISE

You can use this scale when an E7 or E9 chord is indicated.

PROGRESSION #7

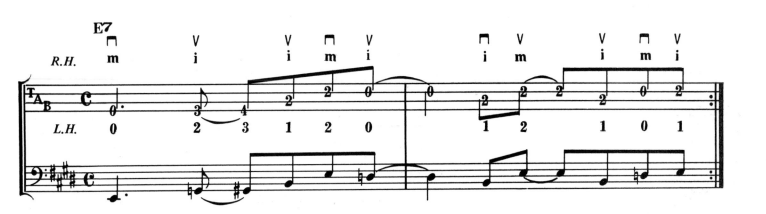

E BLUES SCALE

This is a widely used scale in rock.

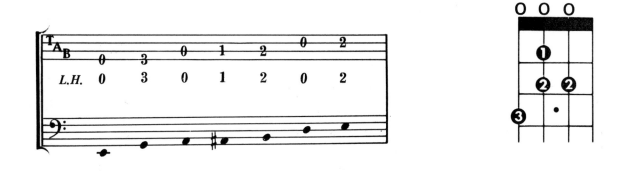

EXERCISE

The notes produced by five out of six open strings on the guitar are found in this scale.

PROGRESSION #8

E NATURAL MINOR SCALE

More frequently used in *legit* or notated music than in rock and jazz, the E natural minor scale is the source scale from which all other E minor scales are derived.

EXERCISE

The next line goes back three hundred years to the composition *Bourrée* by J. S. Bach. Taken from the lute tablature, the line has a unity that transcends time.

PROGRESSION #9

E MINOR JAZZ SCALE

A solid improvisational scale, the E minor jazz scale works well in extended passages where the primary tonality is E minor.

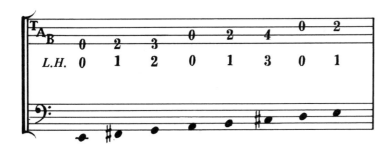

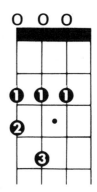

EXERCISE

E MELODIC MINOR SCALE

Although it is infrequently used on the electric bass you should be nonetheless familiar with this scale.

EXERCISE

The C Scales

C MAJOR SCALE

If you ever make music with a keyboard player, this scale will definitely get a workout. It is the easiest key to play (all the white keys) hence the most popular. In fact, I've played with professional keyboard players who could *only* improvise in the key of C.

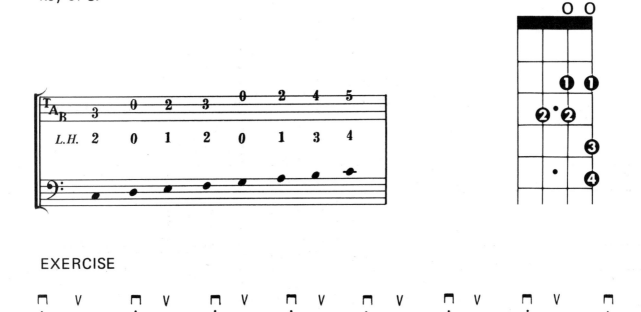

EXERCISE

The C major scale is repeatedly used for lines in soul and pop-style tunes.

PROGRESSION #10

C 6TH SCALE

This is an essential improvisational scale.

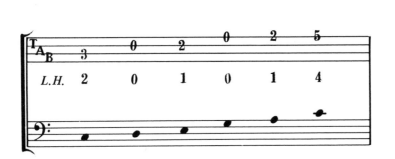

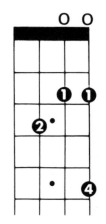

EXERCISE

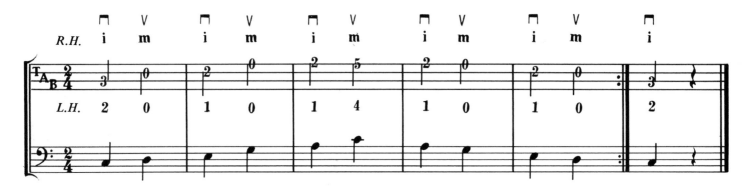

The C 6th scale, played with a C major or C6 chord, can provide a solid harmonic and rhythmic background for horns and voices.

PROGRESSION #11

C 7TH SCALE

When the keyboard player graduates from the C major scale, this is usually the first (and sometimes last) improvisational scale he learns. You better know it, too. The left hand changes position on the 1st string.

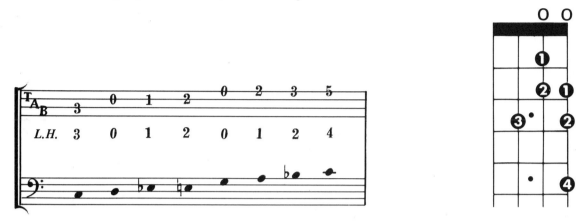

EXERCISE

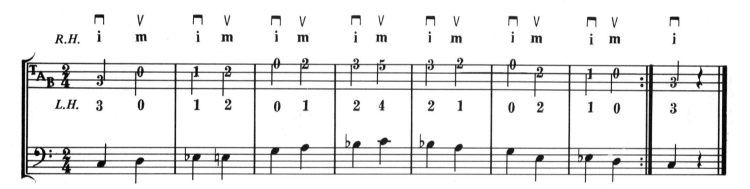

This scale provides solid, funky, effective lines worthy of any straight-ahead, up-tempo boogie in C.

PROGRESSION #12

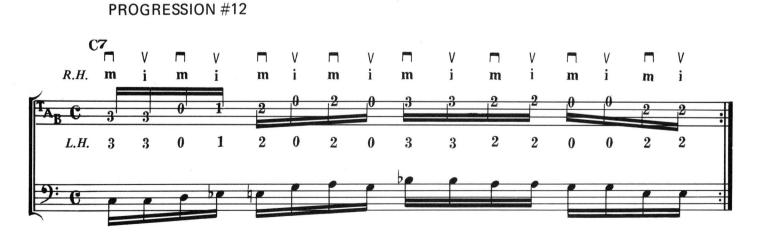

C BLUES SCALE

A necessary scale to know, especially in keyboard bands.

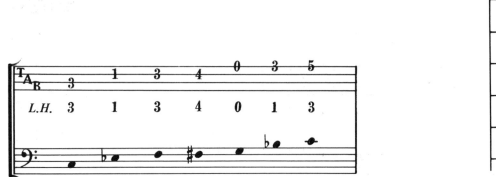
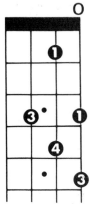

EXERCISE

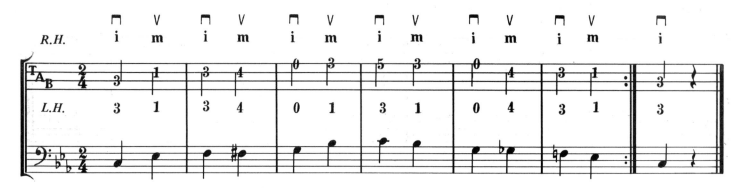

With a tight drummer, this progression has a persuasive rhythmic intensity.

PROGRESSION #13

C MINOR JAZZ SCALE

To execute this scale in open position, the left hand must change positions when fingering the 1st string.

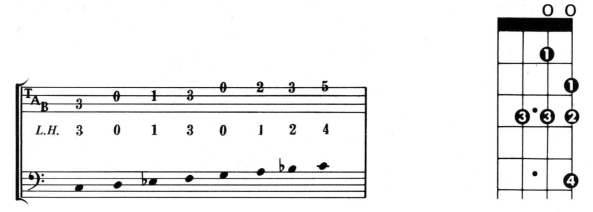

EXERCISE

The G Scales

G MAJOR SCALE

A favorite guitar key, G major is important to know.

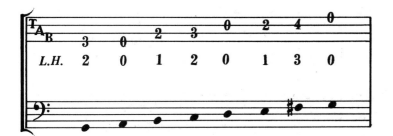

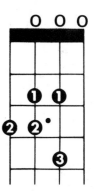

EXERCISE

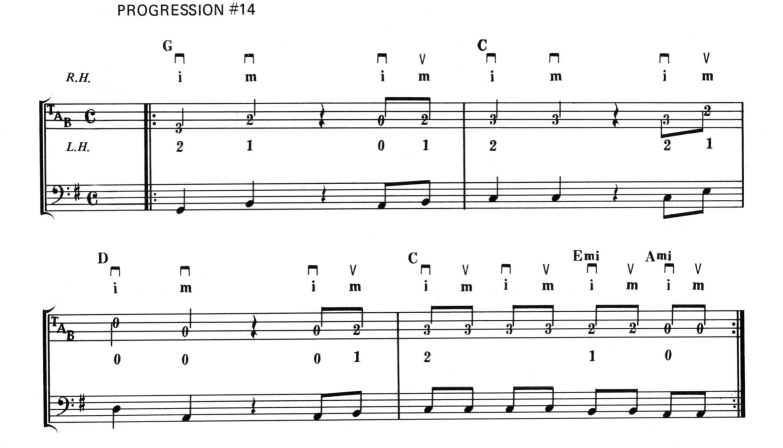

Play the next progression up-tempo with the notes as detached as possible (stacatto).

PROGRESSION #14

G 6TH SCALE

The G 6th scale in open position possesses a unique flowing quality.

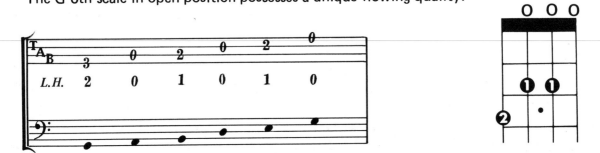

EXERCISE

Using this scale as the basis for a line, the bass easily sustains interest. It works best with a G or G6 chord.

PROGRESSION #15

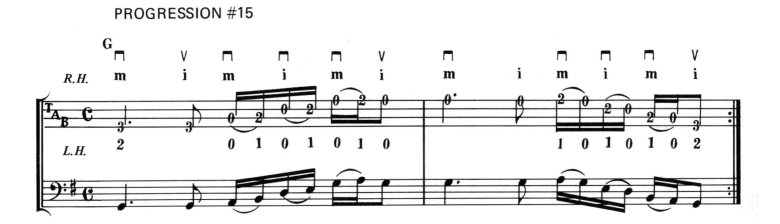

G 7TH SCALE

The structure of the G 7th scale is similar to the C 7th scale. Progression #16 illustrates this.

EXERCISE

This scale works with any G7 or G9 chord. When combined with the C 7th scale, it can cook. Play this progression at a fast tempo (speed).

PROGRESSION #16

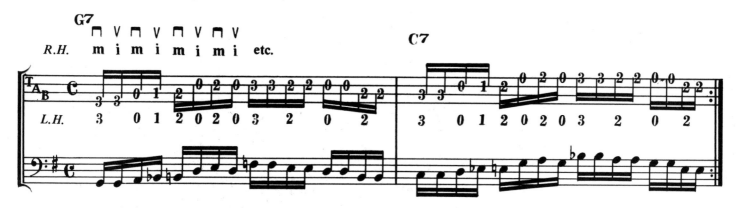

G BLUES SCALE

The blues scale is the only indigenous American scale. G is one of the more important blues scales to be familiar with.

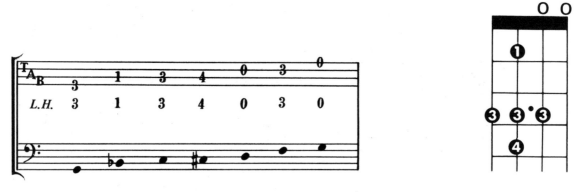

EXERCISE

This scale is used with a variety of G chords including G7, G9, Gmi7, Gmi9.

PROGRESSION #17

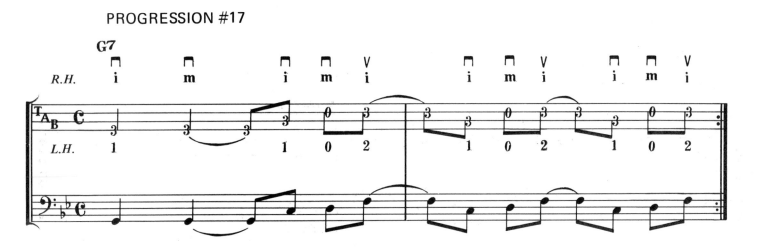

G NATURAL MINOR SCALE

This is the scale from which all the other G minor scales are drawn.

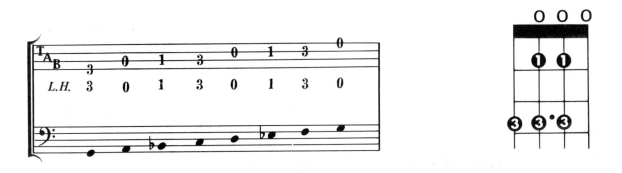

EXERCISE

G MINOR JAZZ SCALE

Many expressive lines have been created with this scale. It's the same as the G natural minor scale, only the sixth tone is raised (E ♮). Compare the two:

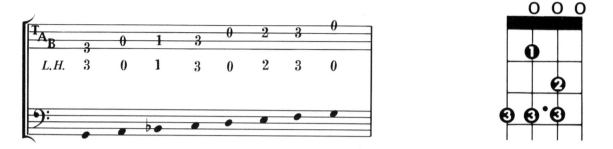

EXERCISE

The raised sixth tone in this scale enables you to play it with the important A minor and C major chords.

PROGRESSION #18

G MELODIC MINOR SCALE

EXERCISE

The B♭ Scales

B♭ MAJOR SCALE

If you ever work in a horn band, this is one scale you'll have to know. B♭ major is the easiest scale for both saxophones and trumpets to blow.

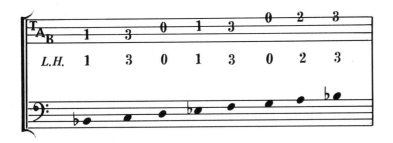

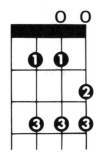

EXERCISE

B♭ 6TH SCALE

This is a charming and effective scale.

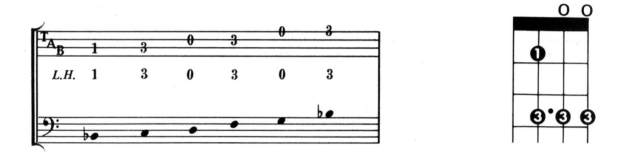

EXERCISE

The next progression illustrates the infinite variety the 6th scales produce.

PROGRESSION #19

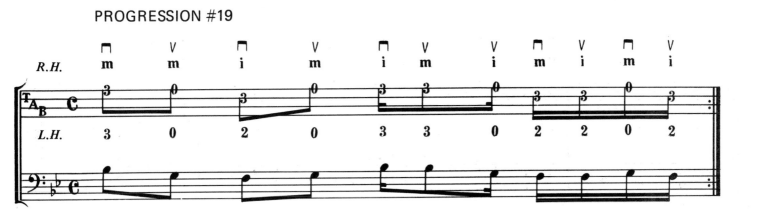

Bb 7TH SCALE

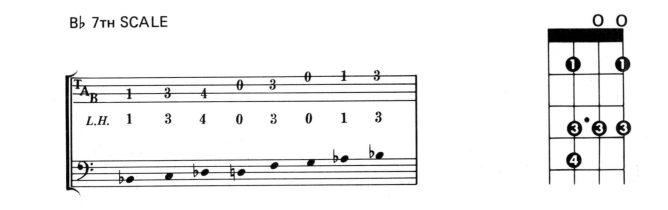

EXERCISE

Bb MINOR JAZZ SCALE

Work on this scale until it sings. It will prove useful later on.

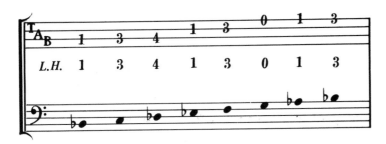
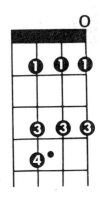

EXERCISE

B♭ MELODIC MINOR SCALE

A little fancy finger-work on the 2nd string is provided by this scale.

EXERCISE

The F Scales

F MAJOR SCALE

This is another favorite horn key. You'll find many soul tunes recorded and performed in F major.

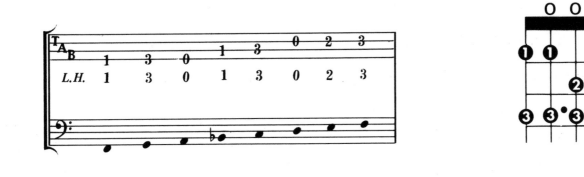

EXERCISE

F 6TH SCALE

The F 6th scale works well in open position.

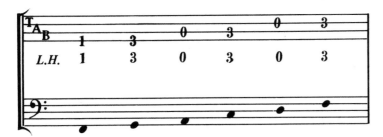

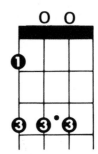

EXERCISE

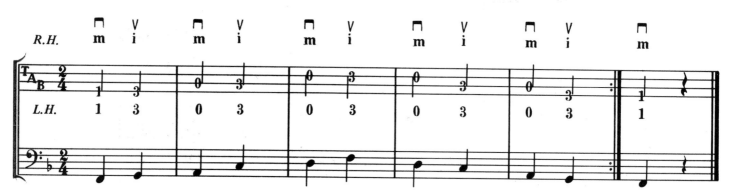

The open strings make a lengthy series of slurs possible. The line surges from their momentum.

PROGRESSION #20

F 7TH SCALE

Get into a band with a harmonica player and you'll be using this scale a lot.

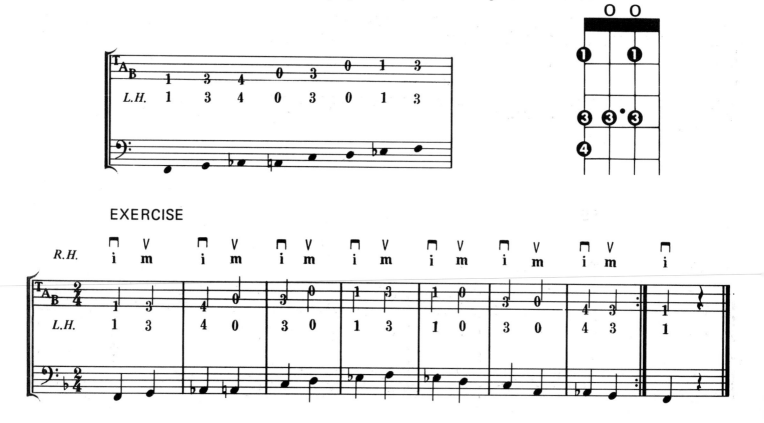

EXERCISE

F MINOR JAZZ SCALE

EXERCISE

F MELODIC MINOR SCALE

EXERCISE

The Chromatic Scale

The chromatic scale is a good open string scale for left hand calisthenics. Ancient in origin, a knowledge of it gives you an excellent feel for the first four frets of the bass. In this scale, the finger and the fret numbers are the same throughout. For example, the 1st finger is only used behind the 1st fret, the 2nd finger behind the 2nd fret, the 3rd finger behind the 3rd fret, and the 4th behind the 4th. The diagram makes this easier to understand.

EXERCISE

SCALES IN CLOSED POSITION

The scales and lines in this section are intended for the advanced to professional bass player. You should have a thorough grasp of the preceding section before starting.

A scale is said to be in closed position when there are no open or unstopped (unfingered) strings used. In general, string players prefer to play in closed position since this technique provides additional control over the duration of the notes. Closed position playing makes punchy, stacatto notes possible by releasing the pressure of the fretting finger. Finger vibrato can also be applied. Further, it allows any riff, scale, or line that you learn to be easily transposed to other keys. This makes any idea you learn in one key instantly applicable to any other key simply by shifting the left hand position.

One Octave Scales

For day to day gigging, one octave scales are the most used. The same length as the scales in the preceding section, the position of the left hand is stationary throughout making them extremely practical in performing situations.

The Major Scales

Before learning our first closed position scale, play the G major scale you already know: the G major scale using open strings.

G MAJOR SCALE IN OPEN POSITION

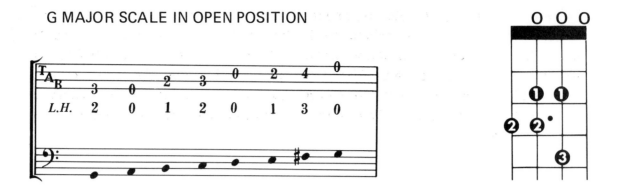

Here's the same scale in closed position. The open strings are eliminated by bringing the 4th finger of the left hand into play. Compare the two. There are no little *o*'s in this one.

G MAJOR SCALE IN CLOSED POSITION

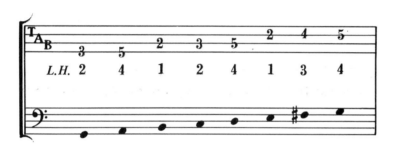
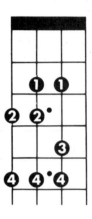

Fingering the G major scale in closed position converts it into a movable major scale.

MOVABLE MAJOR SCALE

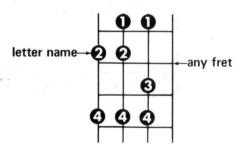

This means that using the same left hand and right hand fingerings you can play about 12 major scales! To understand where to locate these major scales, examine the illustrated note chart:

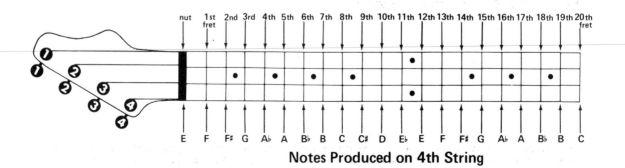

Notes Produced on 4th String

The letters (E, F, F#, G, etc.) represent the notes produced by the 4th string* at various frets. When you fret behind the 3rd fret the 4th string produces the note G; behind the 5th fret the 4th string produces the note A; behind the 8th fret, C; behind the 10th fret, D; etc. The letter name of this movable major scale is determined by the position the *2nd* finger takes on the 4th string. For example, when the *2nd* finger is behind the 4th fret, the string produces A♭. Thus, you have an A♭ major scale.

A♭ MAJOR SCALE

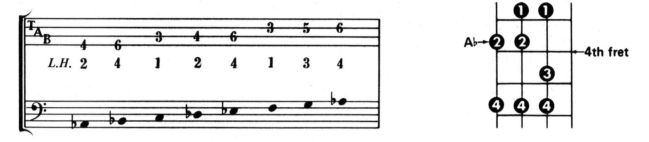

When the *2nd* finger is behind the 5th fret, the 4th string produces A. So you have an A major scale.

A MAJOR SCALE

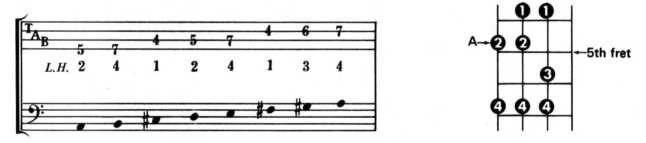

You can play this major scale behind any fret (all the way up to the 18th fret!) Just remember: the letter name of the scale is determined by the position the *2nd* finger takes on the 4th string. To make sure you understand how and where to locate the movable major scale, play the following scales in exercise form. The left hand fingering is identical in every scale.

*Bass strings are numbered from 1 to 4 starting with the highest sounding string (1st string) and going to the lowest sounding string (4th string). The string physically closest to you when you play is the 4th string.

Bb MAJOR SCALE

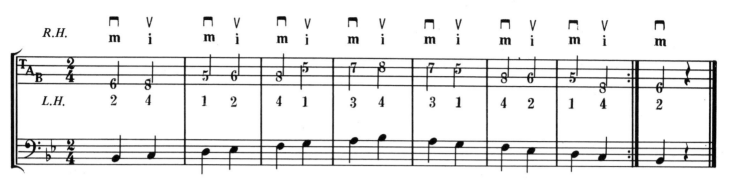

C MAJOR SCALE

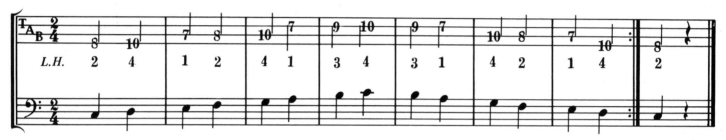

D MAJOR SCALE

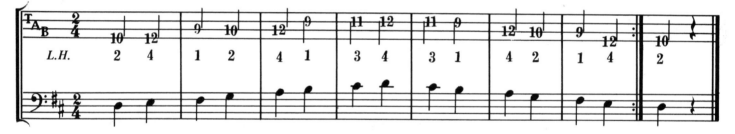

THIRDS IN A

Here's a wonderful exercise in thirds to play using this new scale.

To play this exercise in B♭ you simply move the entire formation up one fret. It makes transposing so easy.

THIRDS IN B♭

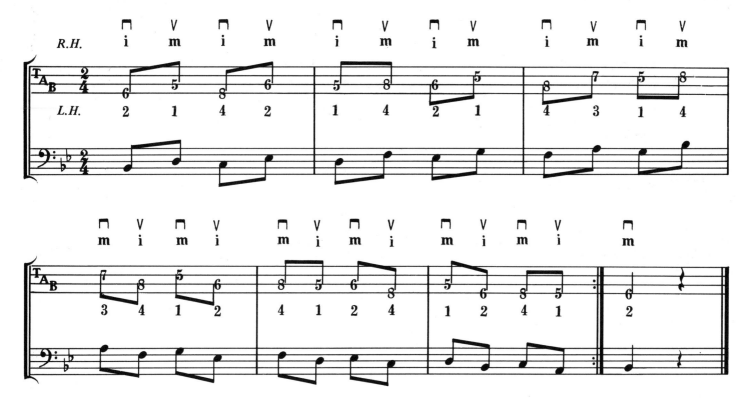

When the scales get as high on the fingerboard as C and D major, the left hand fingering becomes constricted. Also, one of the bass's best registers (the low notes) is completely absent or highly restricted. Try hitting the low G when you're playing in C way up at the 8th fret. Often, it's better to start the C scale on the 3rd string. By knowing the notes produced by the 3rd string, you can easily learn another series of major scales. Examine the note chart.

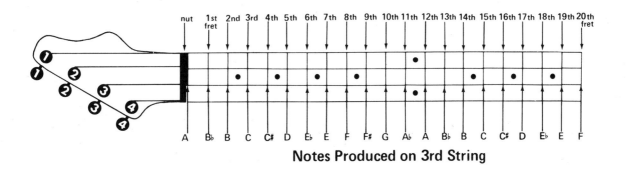

Notes Produced on 3rd String

The letters (A, B♭, B, C, etc.) stand for the notes produced by the 3rd string at various frets. For example, the 3rd string open produces the note A; when you push down behind the 1st fret the 3rd string produces B♭, behind the 3rd fret the 3rd string produces C; etc.

To learn this series of major scales, first play the C major scale from the first section.

C MAJOR SCALE IN OPEN POSITION

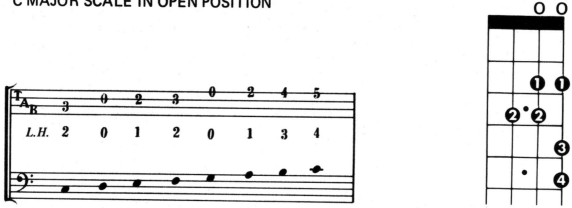

By using the 4th finger of the left hand, no open strings are in the scale. (This scale is really the same as the G major scale except that you start it on the 3rd string rather than the 4th.)

C MAJOR SCALE IN CLOSED POSITION

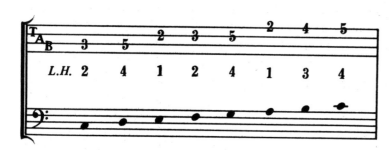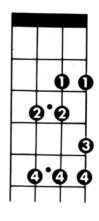

Fingering the C major scale in closed position converts it into a movable major scale.

MOVABLE MAJOR SCALE

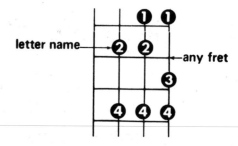

The letter name of this movable major scale is determined by the position the *2nd* finger takes on the 3rd string. For example, when the *2nd* finger is behind the 4th fret, the 3rd string produces C#. Thus, you have a C# major scale.

C# MAJOR SCALE

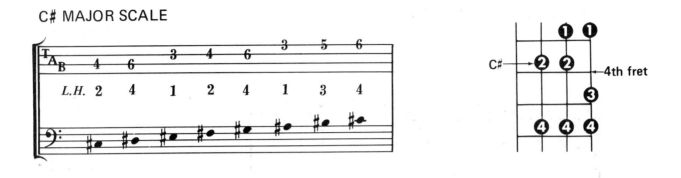

When the *2nd* finger is behind the 5th fret the 3rd string produces D. So you have a D major scale.

D MAJOR SCALE

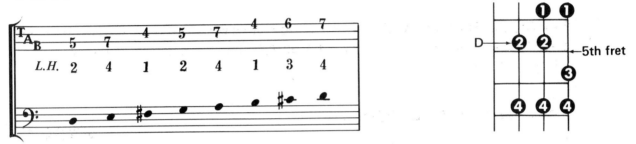

You can play this major scale behind any fret (all the way up to the 18th fret!). Just remember: the letter name of the scale is determined by the position the *2nd* finger takes on the 3rd string.

Play this exercise in thirds for further practice. Try it also in C, E, and F.

THIRDS IN D

What follows are useful and popular lines which make use of the major scale. The first progression is a standard, and you should be able to play it in any key. It's known as the *turn-around*.

PROGRESSION #1

Entire songs are structured around a catchy bass line, such as this next one fashioned out of the A major scale.

PROGRESSION #2

This next progression illustrates an harmonic movement known as the circle of fourths. Every major scale is used.

PROGRESSION #3

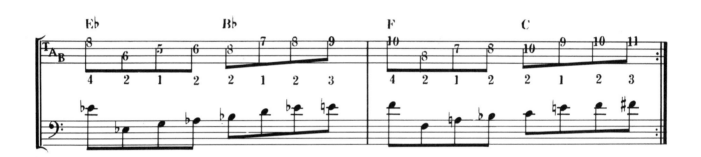

Here's a progression lifted right out of the circle of fourths. With a bass line like this you don't even need words for the song.

PROGRESSION #4

The more usual harmonic movement is in fifths rather than fourths. You should know, or at least be familiar with, the circle of fifths.

PROGRESSION #5

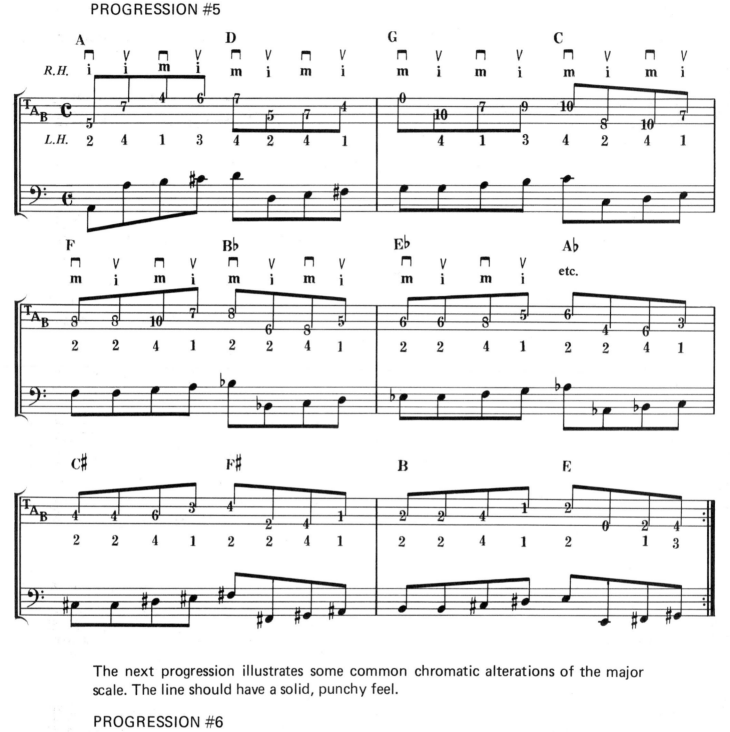

The next progression illustrates some common chromatic alterations of the major scale. The line should have a solid, punchy feel.

PROGRESSION #6

This last progression is another functional exercise in thirds. Like the previous ones, practice it in several other keys.

PROGRESSION #7

The Sixth Scales

Finger and play this familiar G 6th scale using open strings.

G 6TH SCALE IN OPEN POSITION

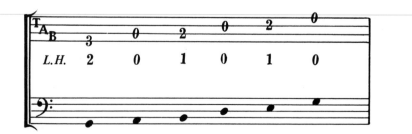

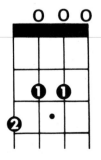

The 4th finger of the left hand eliminates the open strings.

G 6TH SCALE IN CLOSED POSITION

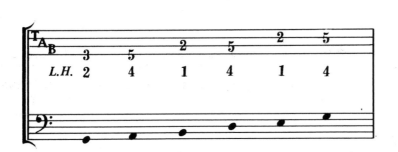

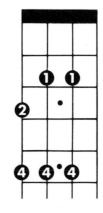

Fingering the G 6th scale in closed position converts it into a movable 6th scale. With this movable scale formation you can play over fifteen 6th scales.

MOVABLE 6TH SCALE

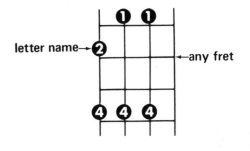

The letter name of this scale is determined by the position the *2nd* finger of the left hand takes on the 4th string.

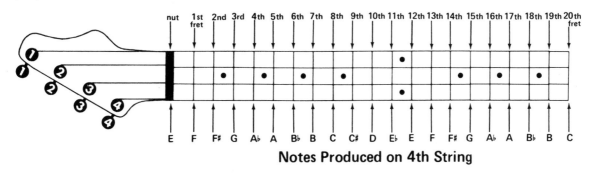

Notes Produced on 4th String

When the *2nd* finger is behind the 3rd fret you have a G 6th scale; behind the 5th fret you have an A 6th scale; behind the 6th fret you have a B♭ 6th scale.

Finger and play the open string C 6th scale that you know.

C 6TH SCALE IN OPEN POSITION

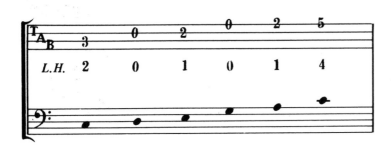

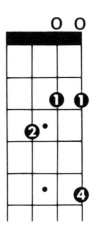

Here's the same scale using no open strings.

C 6TH SCALE IN CLOSED POSITION

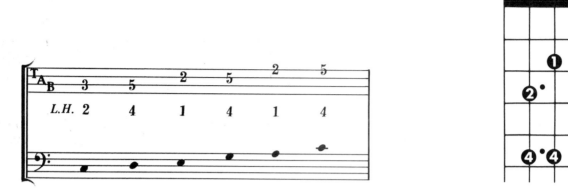

Fingering the C 6th scale in closed position converts it into a movable 6th scale. With this movable scale formation you can play over fifteen 6th scales.

MOVABLE 6TH SCALE

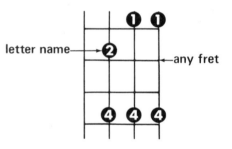

The letter name of this scale is determined by the position the 2nd finger of the left hand takes on the 3rd string.

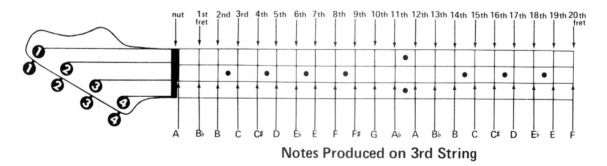

Notes Produced on 3rd String

When the *2nd* finger is behind the 3rd fret you have a C 6th scale; behind the 5th fret you have a D 6th scale; behind the 7th fret you have an E 6th scale.

Lines based on the 6th scale are numerous. The first progression is a slow rocker, over a heavy beat.

PROGRESSION #8

Try this next line on a good fat back*drummer.

PROGRESSION #9

It's hard to go wrong in a dance tune when you use the 6th scale. The scale has a presence, but doesn't demand to be listened to. It is often cast in a supporting role.

*The term "fat back" refers to a style of drumming in which the back of the beat (that is, the 2nd and 4th beats) is heavily accented.

PROGRESSION #10

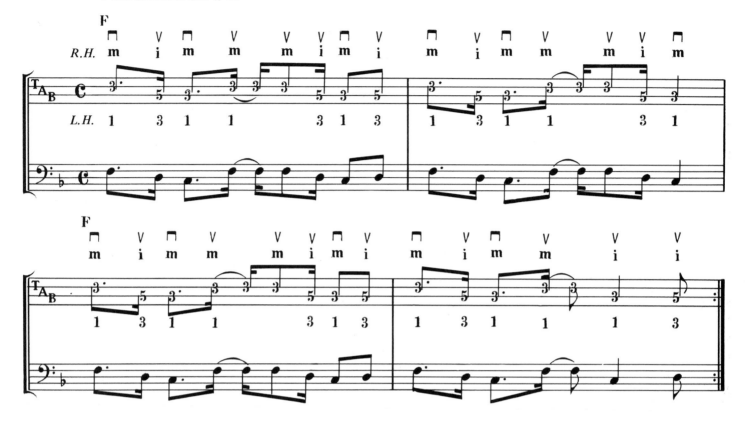

With the 6th scale you can hang onto a rhythm under one chord. This sometimes enhances the melodic instruments.

PROGRESSION #11

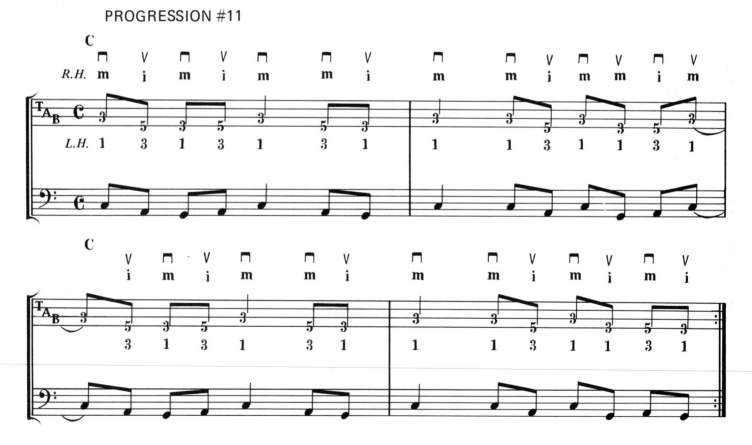

Copping a riff off the 6th scale can get you through a rhythmic blues progression. It's really only one idea multiplied by twelve.

PROGRESSION #12

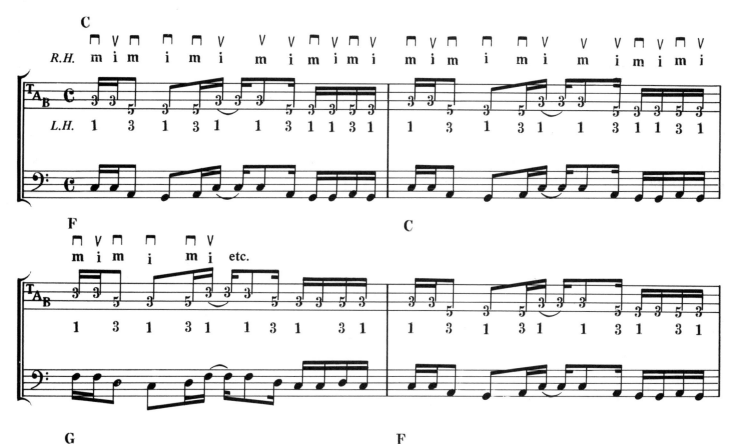

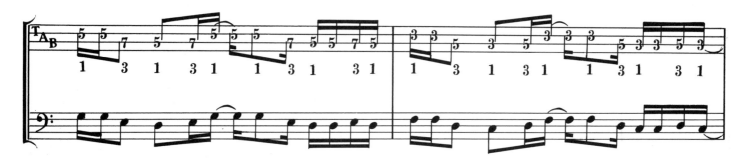

A pleasing modal harmony is nicely supported by a riff drawn from the 6th scale.

The Seventh Scales

Finger and play this G 7th scale using open strings.

G 7TH SCALE IN OPEN POSITION

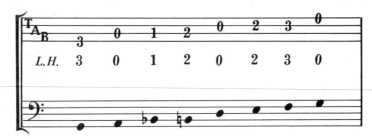

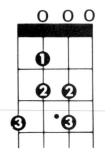

Here's the same scale using no open strings.

G 7TH SCALE IN CLOSED POSITION

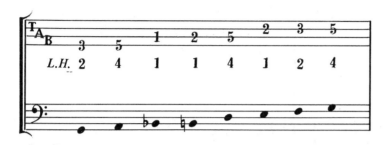
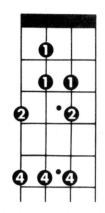

Fingering the G 7th scale in closed position converts it into a movable 7th scale. With this movable scale formation you can play over fifteen 7th scales.

MOVABLE 7TH SCALE

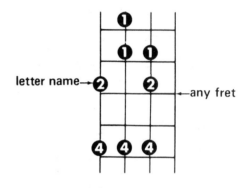

The letter name of this scale is determined by the position the *2nd* finger takes on the 4th string.

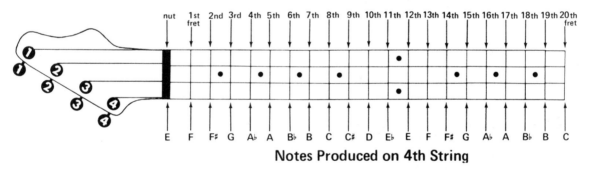

Notes Produced on 4th String

When the *2nd* finger is behind the 3rd fret, you have a G 7th scale; behind the 5th fret you have an A 7th scale; behind the 6th fret you have a B♭ 7th scale.

Finger and play the open string C 7th scale that you know from the 1st section.

C 7TH SCALE IN OPEN POSITION

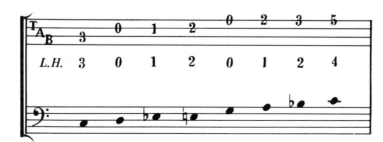
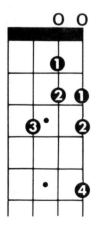

Here's the same scale in a workable form using no open strings.

C 7TH SCALE IN CLOSED POSITION

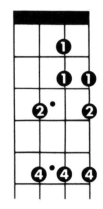

Fingering the C 7th scale in closed position converts it into a movable 7th scale. With this movable scale formation you can play over fifteen 7th scales.

MOVABLE 7TH SCALE

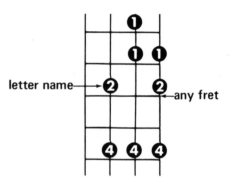

letter name — ② ② — any fret

The letter name of this scale is determined by the position the *2nd* finger of the left hand takes on the 3rd string.

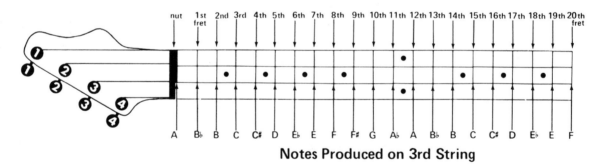

Notes Produced on 3rd String

When the *2nd* finger is behind the 3rd fret, you have a C 7th scale; behind the 5th fret you have a D 7th scale; behind the 7th fret you have an E 7th scale.

The 7th scale is often used in the blues progression. The following blues in G demonstrates an effective usage of this scale:

PROGRESSION #14

An up-tempo blues can turn into a foot stomping rocker with the right bass and rhythm track.

PROGRESSION #15

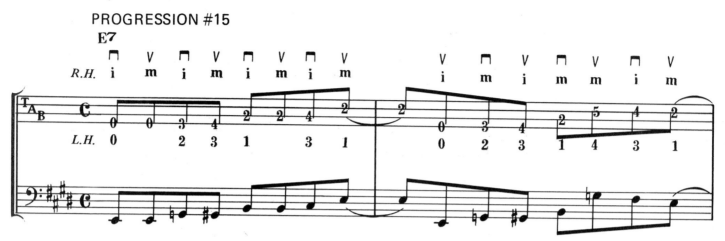

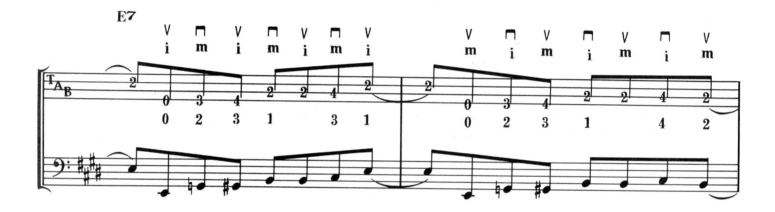

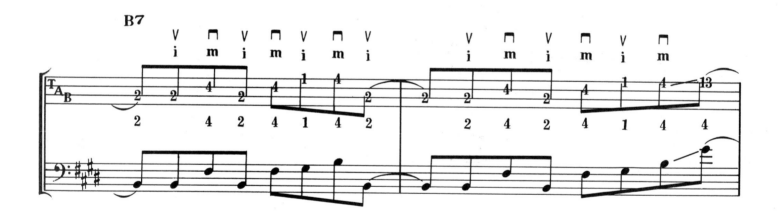

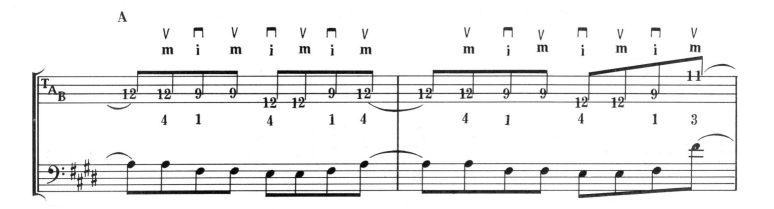

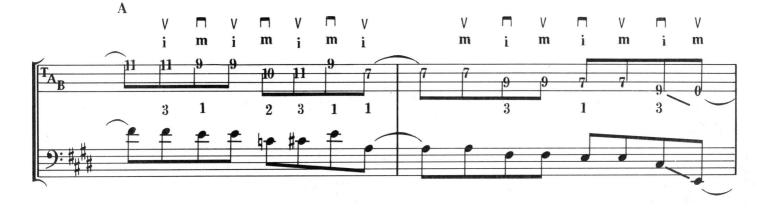

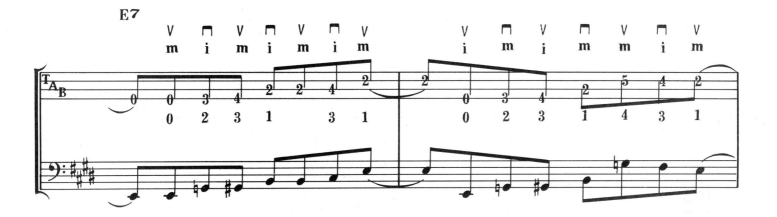

The 7th scale creates such happy lines that it's hard to stop smiling when you play them.

PROGRESSION #16

Learn a good riff and move it around the progression matching the 7th scale with the chord letter name.

PROGRESSION #17

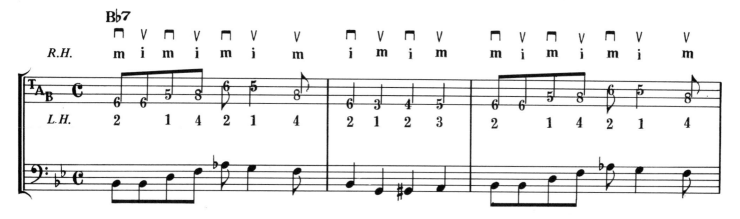

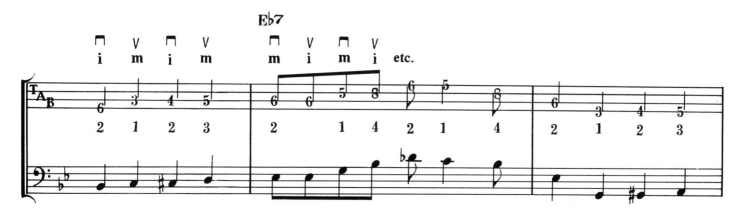

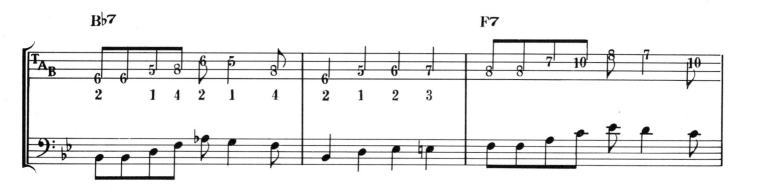

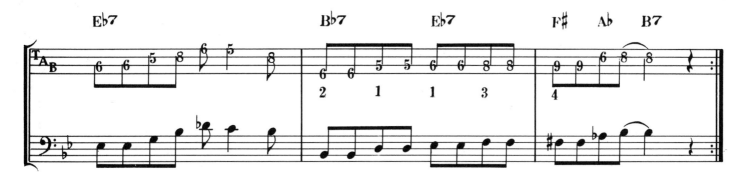

The next line is meant for dancing. It moves nicely through a three chord progression.

PROGRESSION #18

For another example of 7th scales played in riffs, play this progression:

PROGRESSION #19

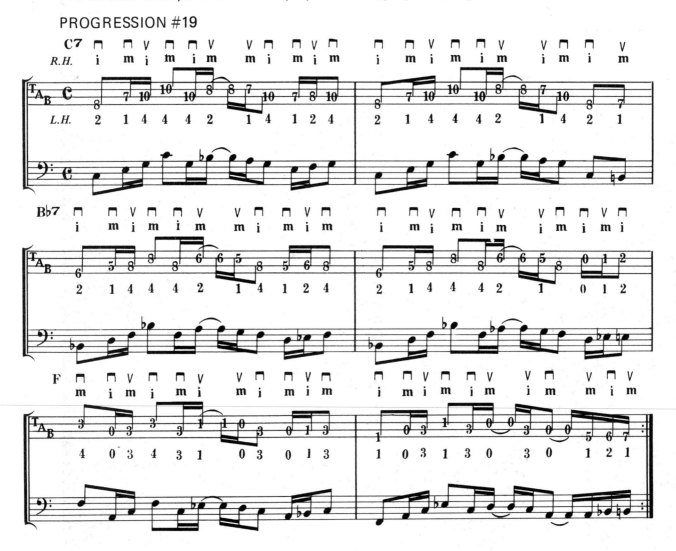

Sometimes you encounter the 7th scale in unexpected places, such as in this soul style line.

PROGRESSION #20

The rhythm of the bass line is critical in a fat back rhythm (where the drummer heavily accents the 2nd and 4th beats). In such a rhythm, the 7th scale adds a taste of funk.

PROGRESSION #21

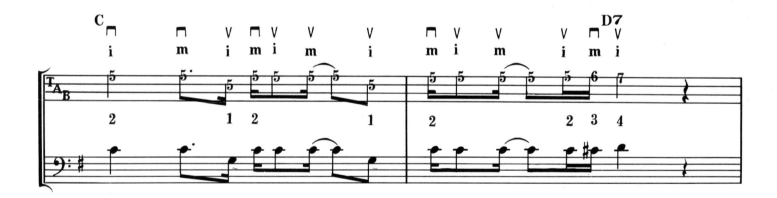

By sharping the 7th, forward motion is created as in this next line.

PROGRESSION #22

Within the same piece different scales are used for variety. Going from one improvisational scale to the next is easy when the ideas are flowing out of your fingers. Both the 6th and the 7th scales are major so they work well together in the next line.

The Blues Scales

Using open strings, the G blues scale is difficult to play fast.

G BLUES SCALE IN OPEN POSITION

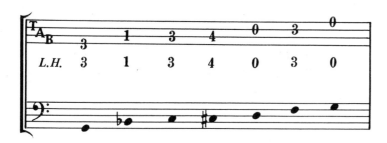
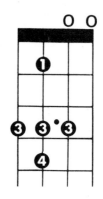

However, in closed position the same scale is much easier to play.

G BLUES SCALE IN CLOSED POSITION

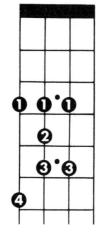

It's really just the E blues scale moved up three frets.

E BLUES SCALE IN OPEN POSITION

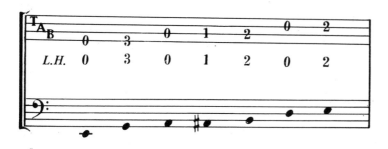
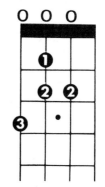

Fingering this blues scale in closed position converts it into a movable blues scale.

With this movable scale formation you can play over fifteen blues scales.

MOVABLE BLUES SCALE

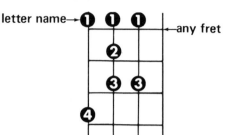

The letter name of this scale is determined by the position the *1st* finger of the left hand takes on the 4th string. This is different than the previous movable scales so take note.

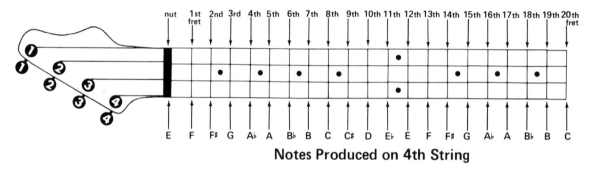

Notes Produced on 4th String

When the *1st* finger is behind the 3rd fret you have a G blues scale; behind the 5th fret you have an A blues scale; behind the 6th fret you have a B♭ blues scale.

The C blues scale using open strings is hard to play in a fast tempo.

C BLUES SCALE IN OPEN POSITION

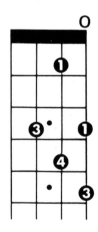

Here's the same scale with a more practical fingering using no open strings.

C BLUES SCALE IN CLOSED POSITION

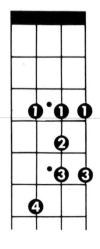

It's really just the A blues scale moved up three frets.

A BLUES SCALE IN OPEN POSITION

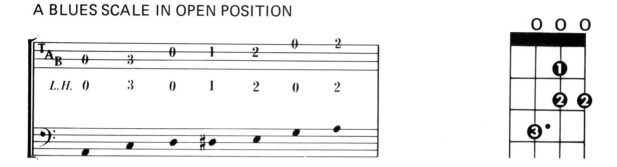

Fingering this blues scale in closed position converts it into a movable blues scale. With this movable scale formation you can play over fifteen blues scales.

MOVABLE BLUES SCALE

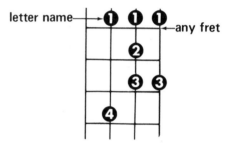

The letter name of this scale is determined by the position the *1st* finger of the left hand takes on the 3rd string.

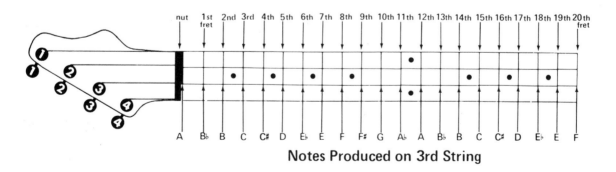

Notes Produced on 3rd String

When the *1st* finger is behind the 3rd fret you have a C blues scale; behind the 5th fret you have a D blues scale; behind the 7th fret you have an E blues scale.

Many fine bass parts have been created from the blues scale, the most popular of the improvisational scales. Sometimes the electric bass and lead guitar play the same line for sudden emphasis in a gutsy blues. Try the next one in G.

PROGRESSION #24

When using the A blues scale, you can occasionally make use of the open 4th string.

PROGRESSION #25

You can also employ the open 4th string with the E blues scale. An important alternate fingering is used in Progression #26.

PROGRESSION #26

Blues scales that start on the 3rd string sometimes use notes from the 4th string as a pick-up as in the next progression. Of course, any of the lines being presented here that use no open strings are highly mobile. This line could be easily played in D or F simply by moving it a few frets in either direction.

PROGRESSION #27

To pick up a low note, you often have to alter the fingering slightly. But you soon fall back into a familiar pattern.

PROGRESSION #28

An interesting variation in the blues scale fingering in the next progression allows you to keep your left hand stationary throughout. In this position, the A blues scale is very similar to the C 6th scale, the relative major.

PROGRESSION #29

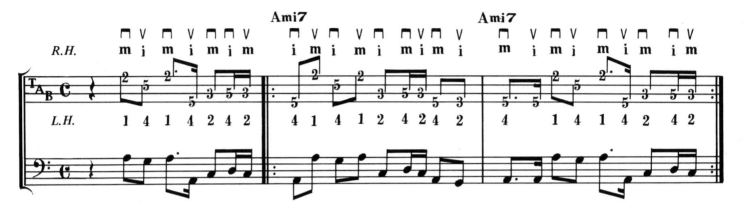

Whether to use the standard fingering of the blues scale really depends on the line. Here we switched fingerings to keep the basic riff in a two fret range.

PROGRESSION #30

Sometimes so few notes are stated in a riff that it's difficult to tell which scale is being used. However, the blues scale provides the basis for the fingering as is illustrated by the next five progressions.

PROGRESSION #31

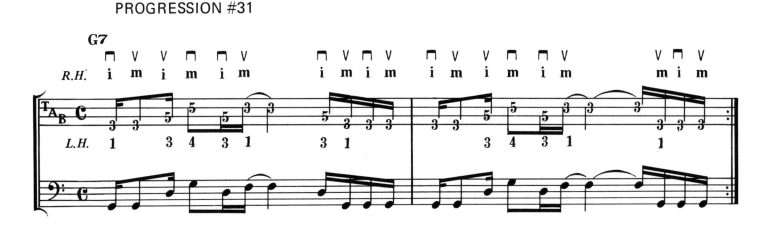

The following line is built on the three most important notes in the blues scale (1, 5, 7):

PROGRESSION #32

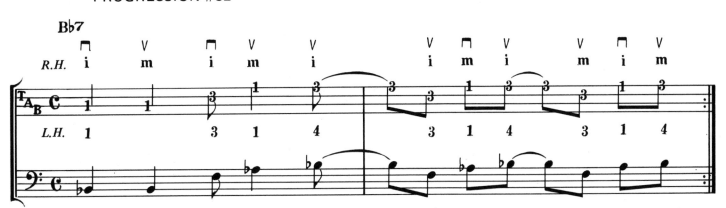

The variations possible with the same three note riff are extensive. Once the idea is stated, it's a simple matter to move it around with the different chords in a progression.

PROGRESSION #33

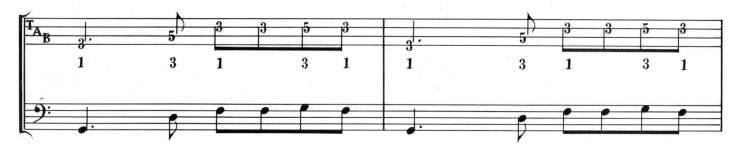

It's difficult to put in a key signature in this type of line since the chordal instruments determine the tonality.

PROGRESSION #34

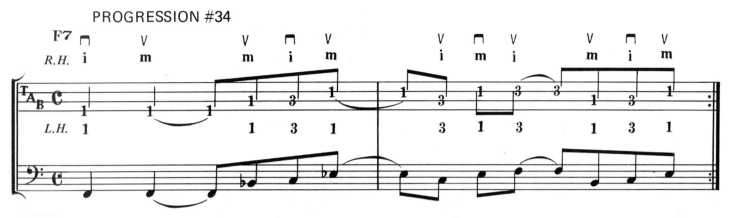

One might think that this next blues progression is in B♭ but it's really in F:

IV/IV/IV/IV/I /I /I /I /V7/IV/I /I.

PROGRESSION #35

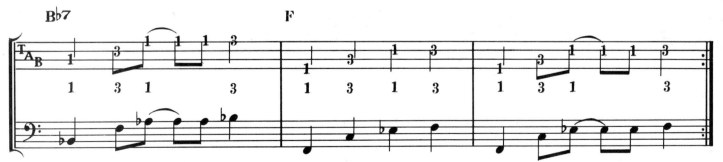

The raised 7th is sometimes used with the blues scale as a chromatic passing tone. Since the raised 7th is characteristic of the major scale and the lowered 7th is characteristic of the minor scale, the tonality of the scale becomes more ambigious. The last two bars are snappy and really unexpected. Using the thumb of the right hand here makes the right hand fingering more natural.

PROGRESSION #36

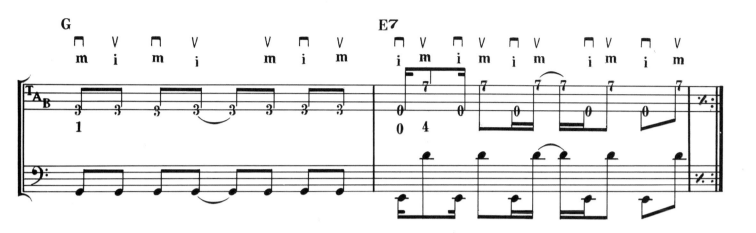

This progression illustrates the sharped 4th and 7th in the blues scale. The line could be played with a G minor 7th chord or a G augmented 9th chord.

PROGRESSION #37

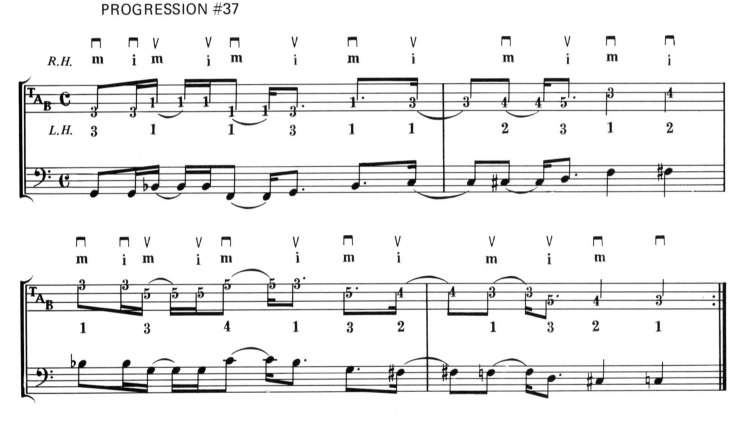

The 7th and the blues scales are often used together creating a definite major feel. Try substituting the thumb for the index finger in measure one.

PROGRESSION #39

Here's a smooth disco line combining the 7th and blues scales effectively.

PROGRESSION #40

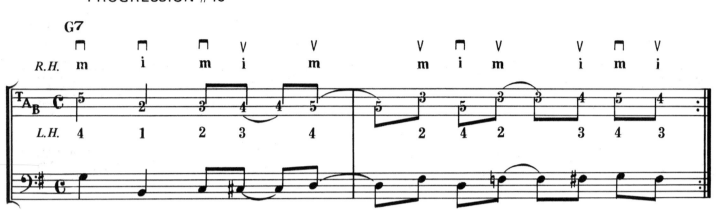

The next line is a slow, funky thing using the A blues scale. The 7th scale makes a humorous entrance in the last bar and determines the tonality.

PROGRESSION #41

The next blues bass line again illustrates the 7th and blues scales played together. Other chromatic passing tones are added for flavor.

PROGRESSION #42

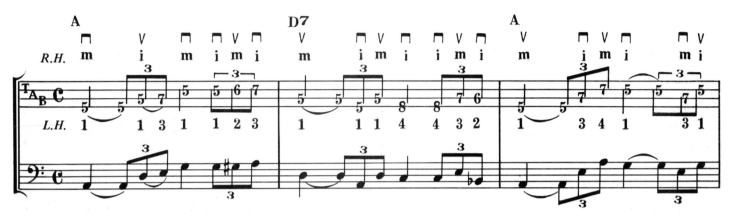

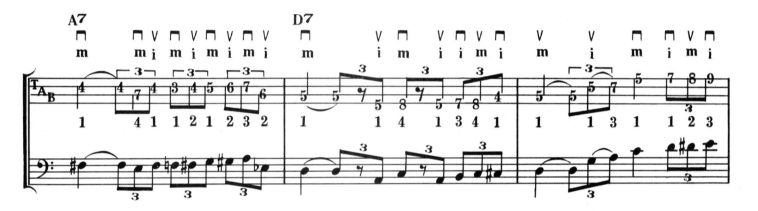

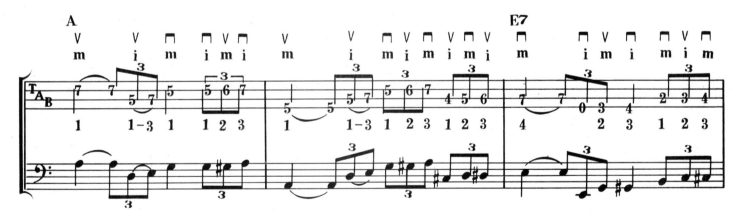

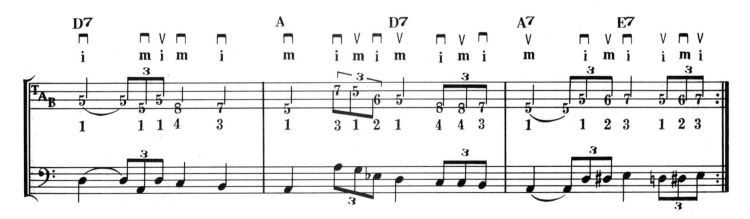

For another example of the 7th and blues scales combined, play this next progression.

PROGRESSION #43

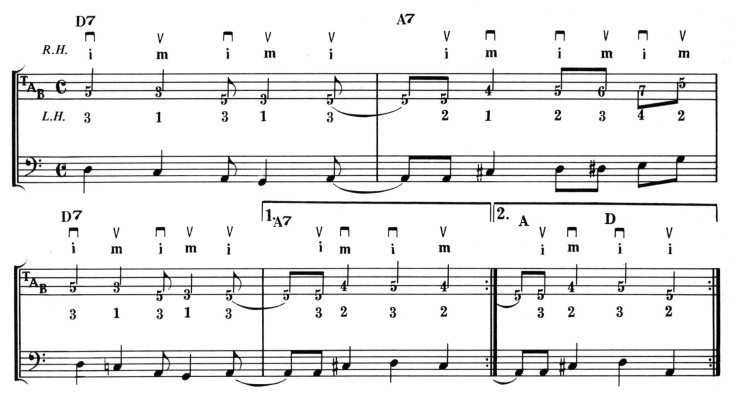

This next up-tempo blues in G provides another example of the blues and 7th scales combined. The sophisticated harmony provides further opportunities for chromaticism.

PROGRESSION #44

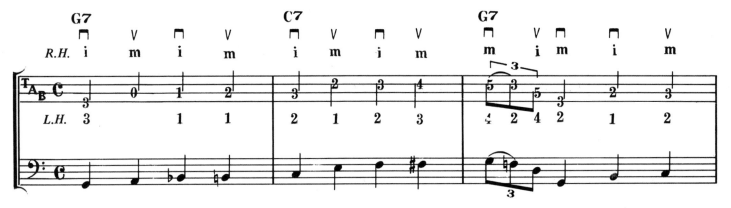

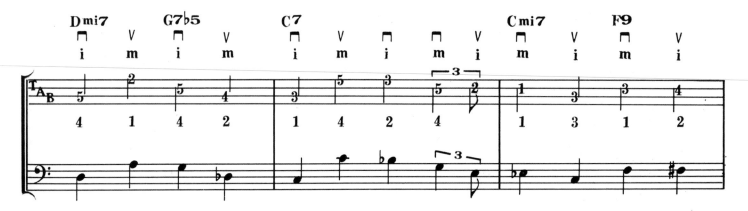

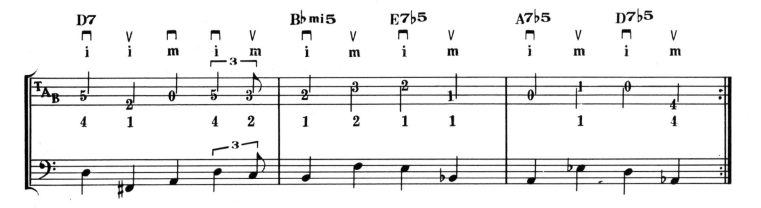

The Natural Minor Scales

Finger and play the G natural minor scale using open strings.

G NATURAL MINOR SCALE IN OPEN POSITION

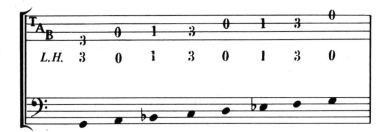

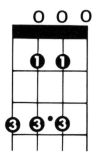

Here's the same scale in closed position.

G NATURAL MINOR SCALE IN CLOSED POSITION

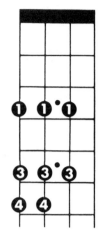

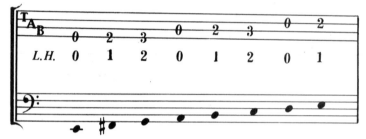

It's really the E natural minor moved up three frets.

E NATURAL MINOR SCALE IN OPEN POSITION

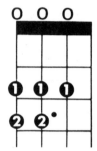

Fingering the natural minor scale in closed position converts it into a movable natural minor scale. With this movable scale formation you can play over fifteen natural minor scales.

MOVABLE NATURAL MINOR SCALE

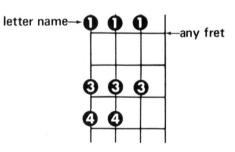

The letter name of this scale is determined by the position the *1st* finger of the left hand takes on the 4th string.

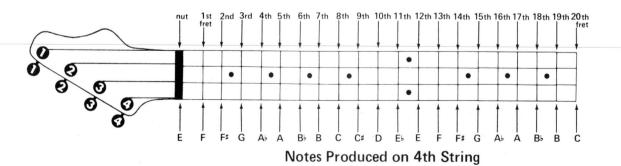

Notes Produced on 4th String

When the *1st* finger is behind the 3rd fret you have a G natural minor scale; behind the 5th fret you have an A natural minor scale; behind the 6th fret you have a B♭ natural minor scale.

Move the same scale over one string and you have a movable natural minor scale starting on the 3rd string.

MOVABLE NATURAL MINOR SCALE

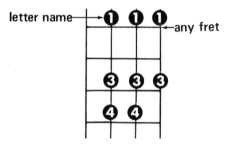

The movable scale is based on the A natural minor scale in open position.

A NATURAL MINOR SCALE IN OPEN POSITION

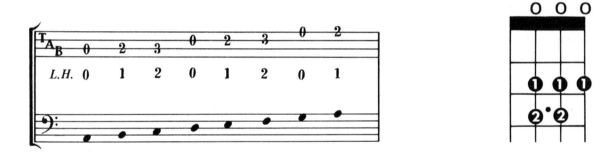

The letter name of the scale is determined by the position the *1st* finger of the left hand takes on the 3rd string.

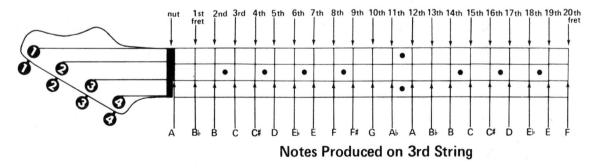

Notes Produced on 3rd String

When the *1st* finger is behind the 3rd fret you have a C natural minor scale; behind the 5th fret you have a D natural minor scale; behind the 7th fret you have an E natural minor scale.

This tasty progression in D minor provides a good example of a line using the natural minor scale. It has a good dance rhythm.

PROGRESSION #45

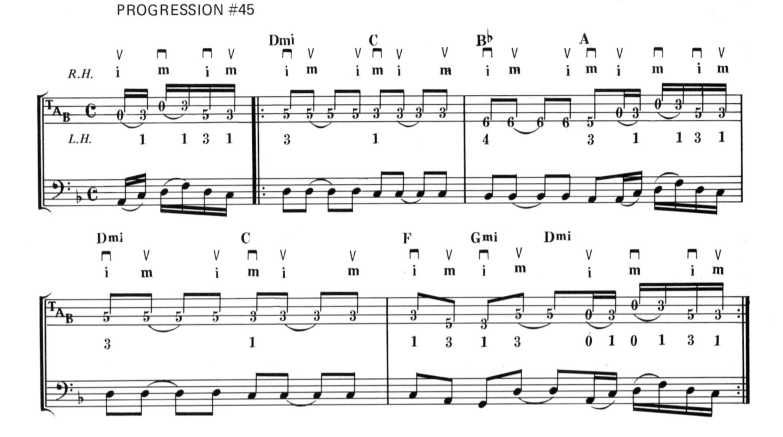

The major-minor tonality of the next progression is not clear until the introduction of the E natural minor scale in bar 5. This much activity in the bass is unusual, and the line at this point is probably doubled by a lead instrument.

PROGRESSION #46

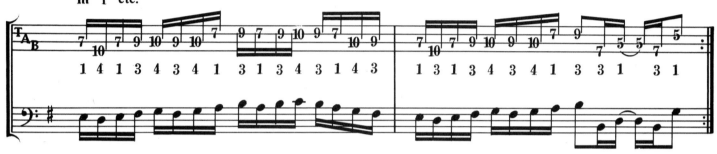

The Minor Jazz Scales

Play the G minor jazz scale using open strings.

G MINOR JAZZ SCALE IN OPEN POSITION

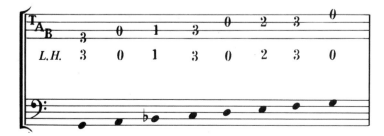

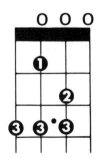

Now try the same scale in closed position. Note the shift in left hand position.

G MINOR JAZZ SCALE IN CLOSED POSITION

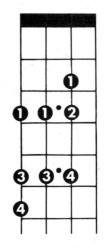

It's really the F minor jazz scale moved up two frets.

F MINOR JAZZ SCALE IN OPEN POSITION

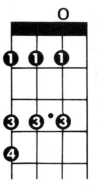

Fingering the minor jazz scale in closed position converts it into a movable minor scale. With this movable scale formation you can play over fifteen minor jazz scales.

MOVABLE MINOR JAZZ SCALE

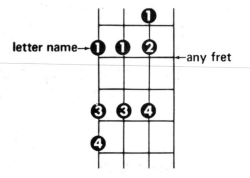

The letter name of this scale is determined by the position the *1st* finger of the left hand takes on the 4th string.

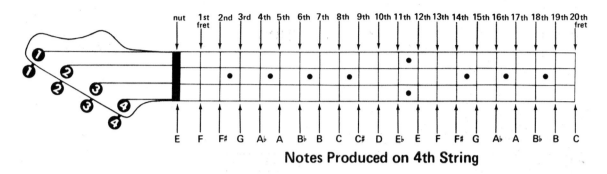

Notes Produced on 4th String

When the *1st* finger is behind the 3rd fret you have a G minor jazz scale; behind the 5th fret you have an A minor jazz scale; behind the 6th fret you have a Bb minor jazz scale.

Play the C minor jazz scale using open strings.

G MINOR JAZZ SCALE IN OPEN POSITION

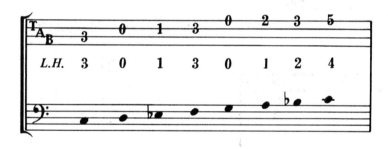

Try the same scale in closed position.

C MINOR JAZZ SCALE IN CLOSED POSITION

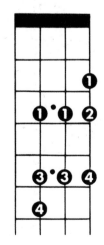

The formation is identical to the Bb minor jazz scale only moved up two frets.

Bb MINOR JAZZ SCALE IN OPEN POSITION

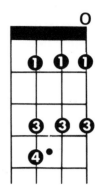

Fingering this minor jazz scale in closed position converts it into a movable minor jazz scale. With this movable scale formation you can play over fifteen minor jazz scales.

MOVABLE MINOR JAZZ SCALE

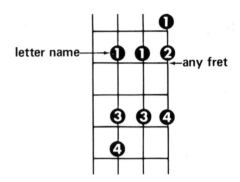

The letter name of this scale is determined by the position the *1st* finger of the left hand takes on the 3rd string.

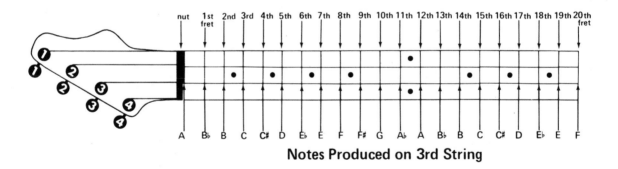

Notes Produced on 3rd String

When the *1st* finger is behind the 3rd fret you have a C minor jazz scale; behind the 5th fret you have a D minor jazz scale; behind the 7th fret you have an E minor jazz scale.

A curious thing about the jazz scale is that it is built on the second degree of the major scale. The A minor jazz scale is really the G major scale starting from the second note A.

PROGRESSION #47

The next progression illustrates the D minor jazz scale.

PROGRESSION #48

The 6th degree from both the C natural minor (Ab) and the C minor jazz (A♮) scales are used in the next progression.

PROGRESSION #49

The Melodic Minor Scales

Finger and play the G melodic minor scale using open strings.

G MELODIC MINOR SCALE IN OPEN POSITION

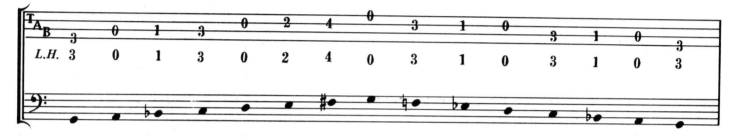

Here's the same scale in closed position.

G MELODIC MINOR SCALE IN CLOSED POSITION

Physically, it's very similar to the F melodic minor scale only moved up two frets.

F MELODIC MINOR SCALE IN OPEN POSITION

Fingering the melodic minor scale in closed position converts it into a movable melodic minor scale. Since the ascending and descending forms are different, two diagrams are necessary.

MOVABLE MELODIC MINOR SCALE

ASCENDING   DESCENDING

The letter name of **this scale is determined by** the position the *1st* finger of the left hand takes on **the 4th string.**

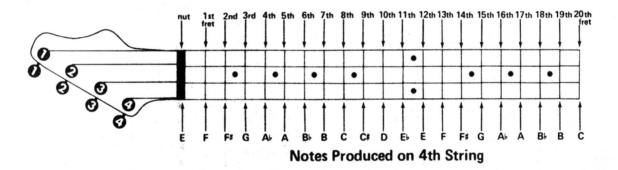

Notes Produced on 4th String

When the *1st* finger is behind the **3rd fret you have a G melodic minor scale; behind the 5th fret you have an A melodic minor scale; behind the 6th fret you have a** B♭ melodic minor scale.

Move the same **scale over one string and you have a movable melodic minor scale** starting on the **3rd string.**

MOVABLE MELODIC MINOR SCALE

ASCENDING   DESCENDING

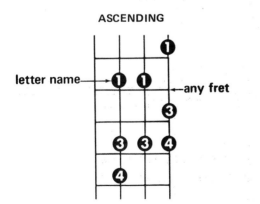

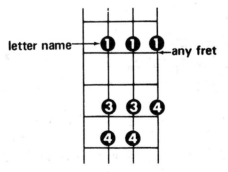

The movable scale is based on the B♭ melodic minor scale in open position.

B♭ MELODIC MINOR SCALE IN OPEN POSITION

The letter name of this scale is determined by the position the *1st* finger of the left hand takes on the 3rd string.

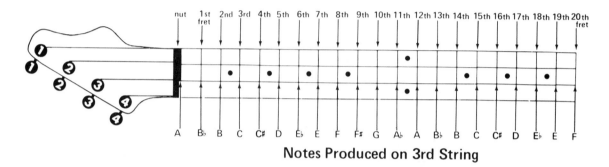

Notes Produced on 3rd String

When the *1st* finger is behind the 3rd fret you have a C melodic minor scale; behind the 5th fret you have a D melodic minor scale; behind the 7th fret you have an E melodic minor scale.

The next progression is a rare example of the melodic minor scale used as the bass line in a rock tune.

PROGRESSION #50

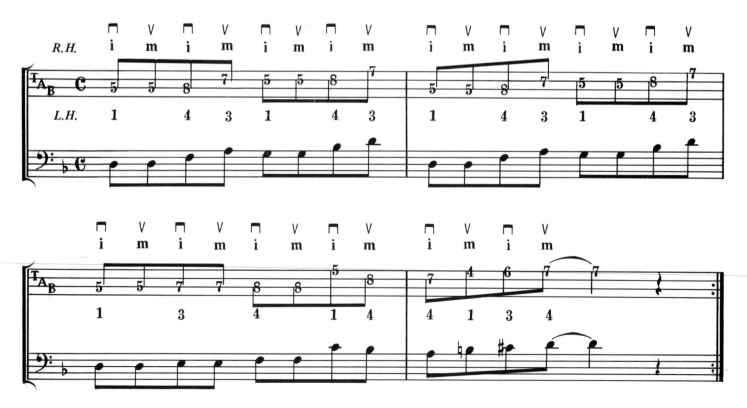

Two Octave Scales

After attaining a moderate degree of left and right hand independence, the student should begin work on the two octave scale in closed position. These scales are not to be over practiced as they are very demanding. If your left hand begins to tire and ache, stop and rest. You might shake the hand vigrously to improve circulation.

No right hand fingerings are indicated as the scales should be practiced starting with the index finger one time and with the middle finger the next (or a pick up-stroke one time and a pick down-stroke the next).

The Major Scales

The two octave G major scale establishes the pattern for the major scales starting on the 4th string. The position of the *2nd* finger of the left hand on the 4th string determines the letter name of the scale.

G MAJOR SCALE

The two octave C major scale establishes the pattern for the major scales starting on the 3rd string. The position of the *2nd* finger of the left hand on the 3rd string determines the letter name of the scale. Alternate left hand fingerings appear in parenthesis.

C MAJOR SCALE

The two major scale patterns traditionally alternate through the cycle of fifths to complete the major scale repertoire.

A MAJOR SCALE

D MAJOR SCALE

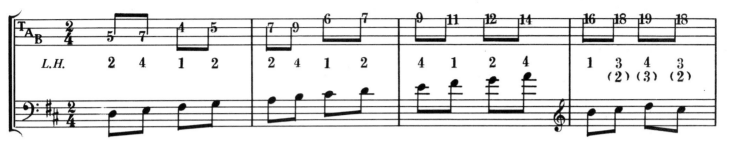

G MAJOR SCALE

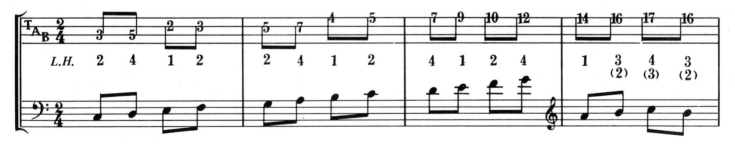

C MAJOR SCALE

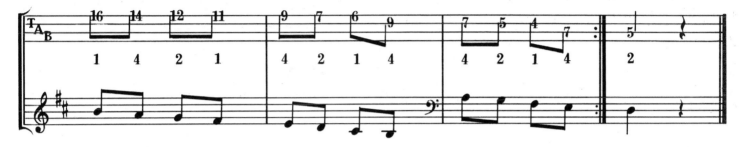

This scale is by necessity unique because of low pitched F on the 4th string.

F MAJOR SCALE

Bb MAJOR SCALE

Eb MAJOR SCALE

Ab MAJOR SCALE

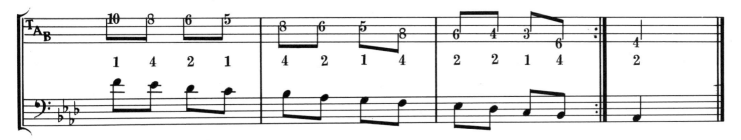

C# MAJOR SCALE

F# MAJOR SCALE

B MAJOR SCALE

Because of the open 4th string, the pattern of the E major scale is used only once.

E MAJOR SCALE

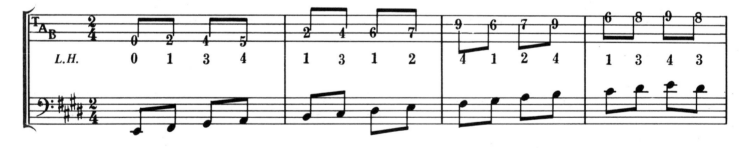

The Sixth Scales

The two octave G 6th scale establishes the pattern for the 6th scales starting on the 4th string. The position of the *1st* finger of the left hand on the 4th string determines the letter name of the scale.

G 6TH SCALE

The two octave C 6th scale fixes the pattern for the 6th scales starting on the 3rd string. The position of the *1st* finger of the left hand on the 3rd string tells you the letter name of the scale. Alternate left hand fingerings appear in parenthesis.

C 6TH SCALE

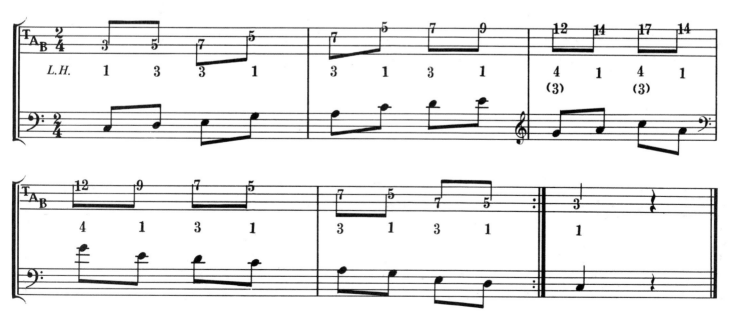

The two forms of the 6th scale alternate through the cycle of fifths to complete the 6th scale repertoire.

A 6TH SCALE

D 6TH SCALE

G 6TH SCALE

C 6TH SCALE

F 6TH SCALE

B♭ 6TH SCALE

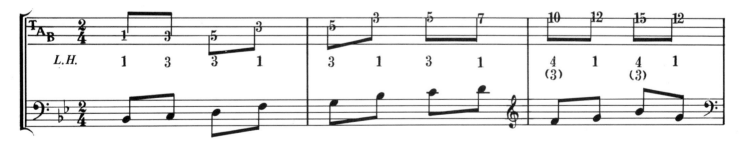

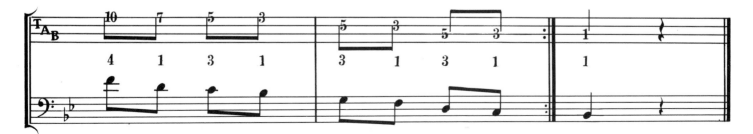

Eb 6TH SCALE

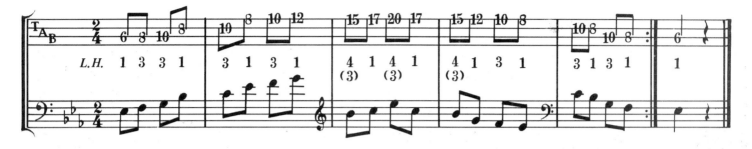

Ab 6TH SCALE

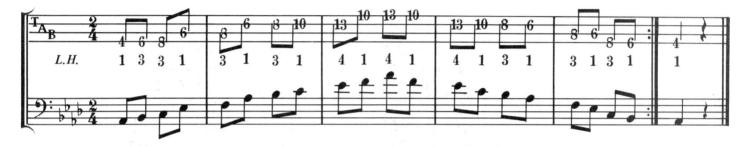

C# 6TH SCALE

F# 6TH SCALE

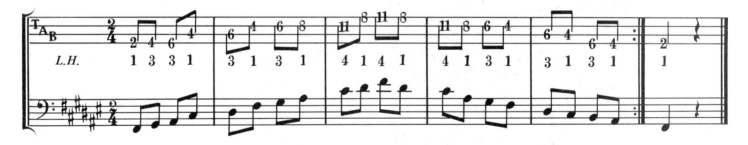

B 6TH SCALE

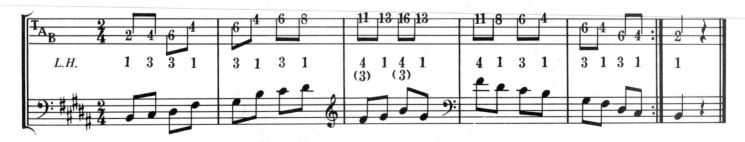

The E 6th scale pattern is used only once because of the open 4th string.

E 6TH SCALE

The Seventh Scales

The two octave G 7th scale fixes the pattern for the 7th scales starting on the 4th string. The position of the *1st* finger of the left hand on the 4th string determines the letter name of the scale.

G 7TH SCALE

The two octave C 7th scale establishes the pattern for the 7th scales starting on the 3rd string. The position of the *1st* finger of the left hand on the 3rd string determines the letter name of the scale.

C 7TH SCALE

The two formations of the 7th scale alternate through the cycle of fifths to complete the 7th scale repertoire.

A 7TH SCALE

D 7TH SCALE

G 7TH SCALE

C 7TH SCALE

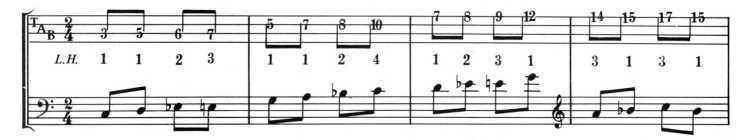

F 7TH SCALE

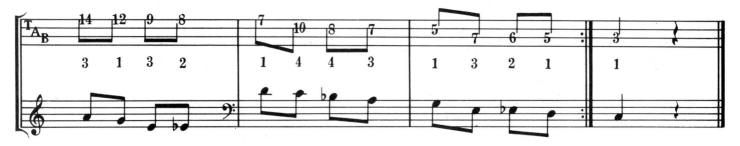

B♭ 7TH SCALE

Eb 7TH SCALE

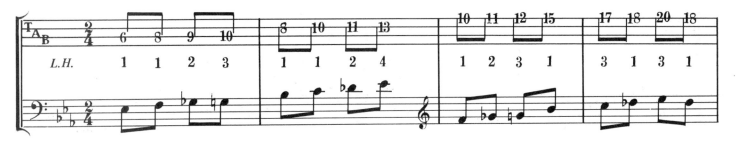

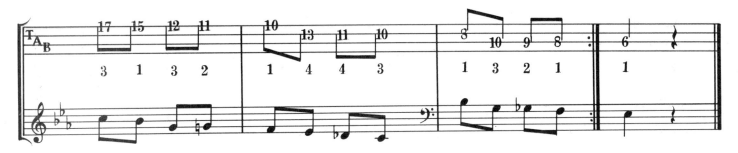

Ab 7TH SCALE

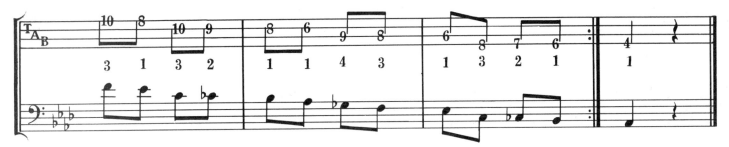

C# 7TH SCALE

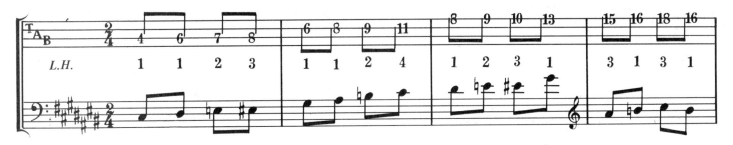

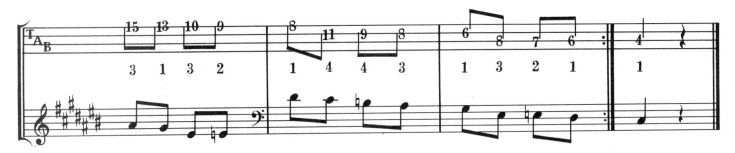

F# 7TH SCALE

B 7TH SCALE

The E 7th scale pattern is used only once because of the open 4th string.

E 7TH SCALE

The Blues Scales

The two octave G blues scale establishes the pattern for the blues scales starting on the 4th string. The position of the *1st* finger of the left hand on the 4th string determines the letter name of the scale.

G BLUES SCALE

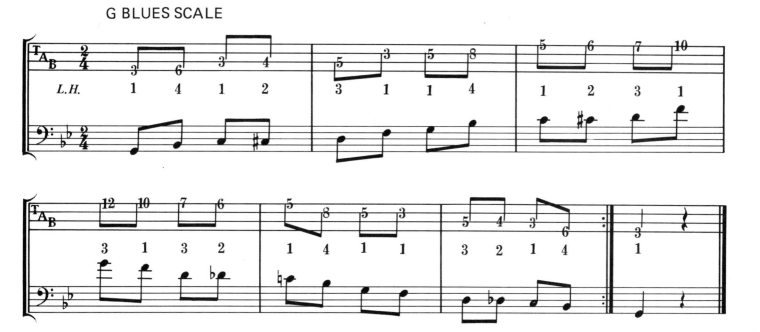

The two octave C blues scale establishes the pattern for the blues scales starting on the 3rd string. The position of the *1st* finger of the left hand on the 3rd string tells you the letter name of the scale. Alternate left hand fingerings appear in parenthesis.

C BLUES SCALE

The two blues scale patterns alternate through the cycle of fifths to complete the blues scale repertoire.

A BLUES SCALE

D BLUES SCALE

G BLUES SCALE

C BLUES SCALE

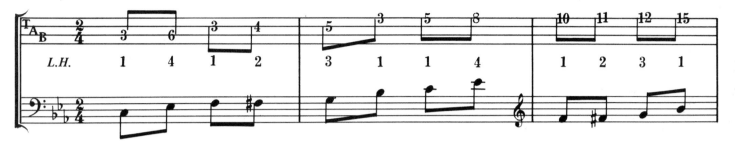

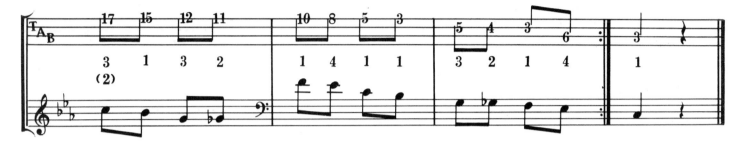

F BLUES SCALE

Bb BLUES SCALE

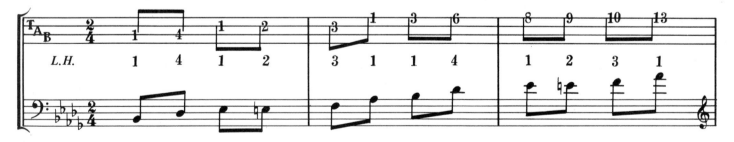

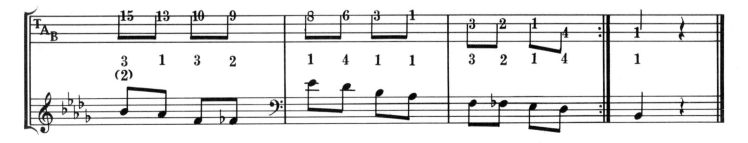

Eb BLUES SCALE

Ab BLUES SCALE

C# BLUES SCALE

F# BLUES SCALE

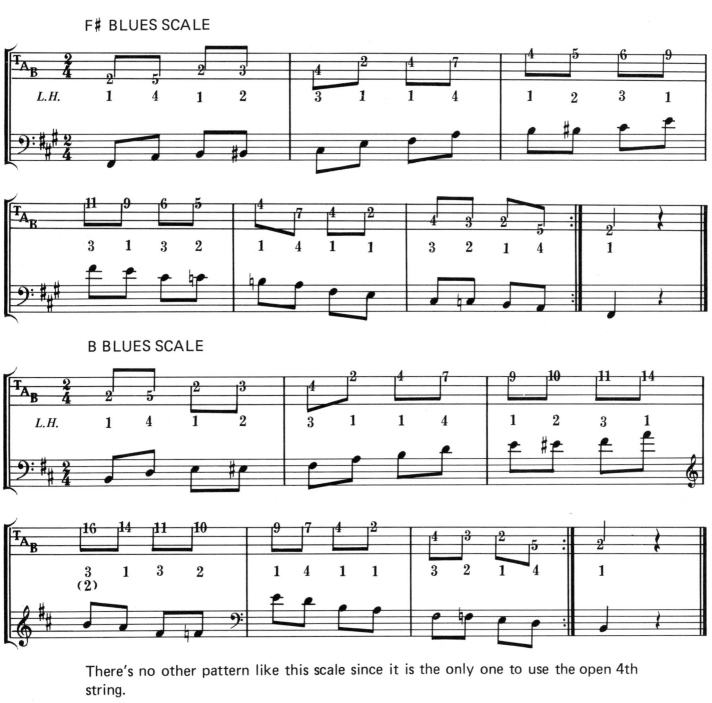

B BLUES SCALE

There's no other pattern like this scale since it is the only one to use the open 4th string.

E BLUES SCALE

The Natural Minor Scales

The two octave G natural minor scale establishes the pattern for the natural minor scales starting on the 4th string. The position of the *1st* finger of the left hand on the 4th string determines the letter name of the scale.

G NATURAL MINOR SCALE

The two octave C natural minor scale establishes the pattern for the natural minor scales starting on the 3rd string. The position of the *1st* finger of the left hand on the 3rd string tells you the letter name of the scale. Alternate left hand fingerings appear in parenthesis.

C NATURAL MINOR SCALE

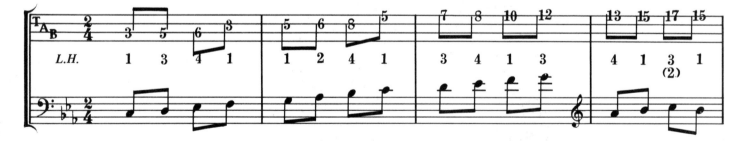

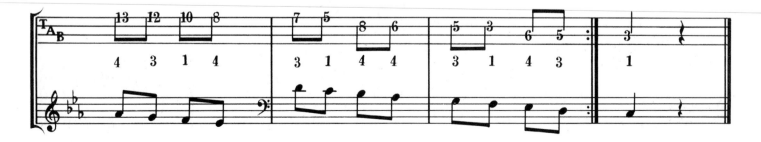

The two natural minor scale patterns alternate through the cycle of fifths to complete the natural minor scale repertoire.

A NATURAL MINOR SCALE

D NATURAL MINOR SCALE

G NATURAL MINOR SCALE

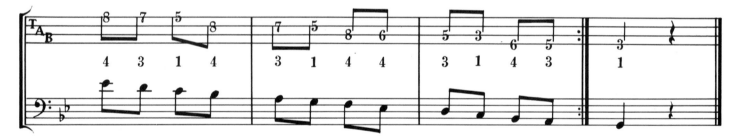

C NATURAL MINOR SCALE

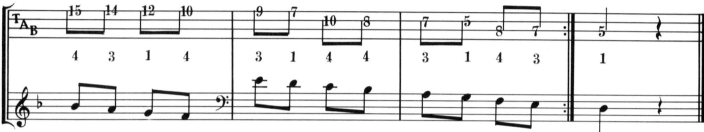

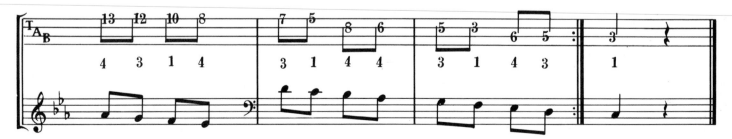

F NATURAL MINOR SCALE

B♭ NATURAL MINOR SCALE

E♭ NATURAL MINOR SCALE

Ab NATURAL MINOR SCALE

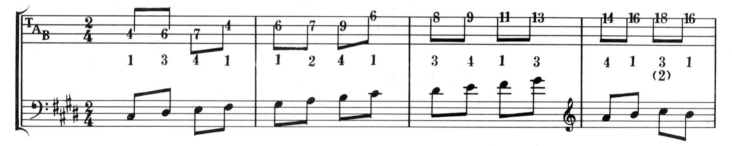

C# NATURAL MINOR SCALE

F# NATURAL MINOR SCALE

B NATURAL MINOR SCALE

The E natural minor scale is unique since it uses the open 4th string.

E NATURAL MINOR SCALE

The Minor Jazz Scales

The two octave G minor jazz scale establishes the pattern for the minor jazz scales starting on the 4th string. The position of the *1st* finger of the left hand on the 4th string tells you the letter name of the scale.

G MINOR JAZZ SCALE

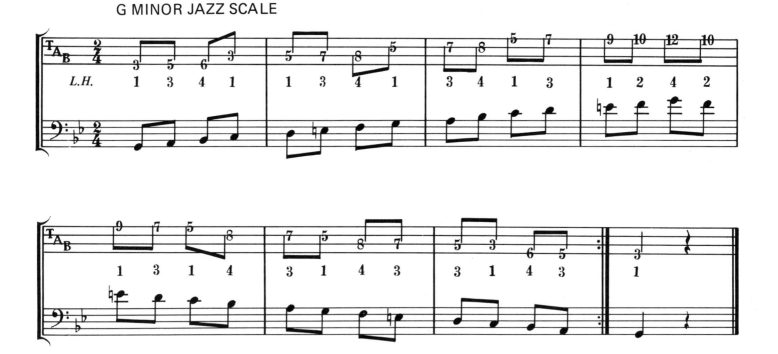

The two octave C minor jazz scale establishes the pattern for the minor jazz scales starting on the 3rd string. The position of the *1st* finger of the left hand on the 3rd string determines the letter name of the scale.

C MINOR JAZZ SCALE

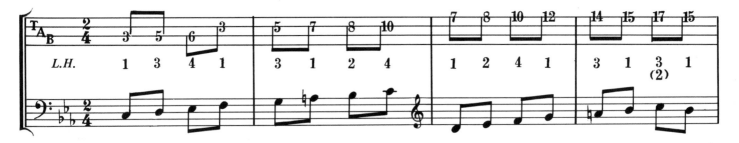

The two minor jazz scale patterns alternate through the cycle of fifths to complete
the minor jazz scale repertoire.

A MINOR JAZZ SCALE

D MINOR JAZZ SCALE

G MINOR JAZZ SCALE

Eb MINOR JAZZ SCALE

Ab MINOR JAZZ SCALE

C# MINOR JAZZ SCALE

F# MINOR JAZZ SCALE

B MINOR JAZZ SCALE

E is the only minor jazz scale that doesn't fit in with the other patterns.

E MINOR JAZZ SCALE

The Harmonic Minor Scales

The two octave G harmonic minor scale establishes the pattern for the harmonic minor scales starting on the 4th string. The position of the *1st* finger of the left hand on the 4th string determines the letter name of the scale.

G HARMONIC MINOR SCALE

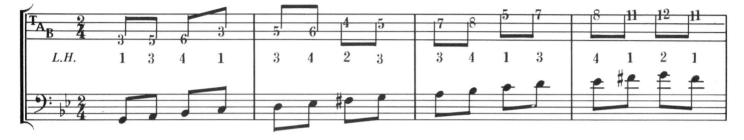

The two octave C harmonic minor scale establishes the pattern for the harmonic minor scales starting on the 3rd string. The position of the *1st* finger of the left hand on the 3rd string tells you the letter name of the scale.

C HARMONIC MINOR SCALE

The two harmonic minor scale patterns alternate through the cycle of fifths to complete the harmonic minor scale repertoire.

A HARMONIC MINOR SCALE

D HARMONIC MINOR SCALE

G HARMONIC MINOR SCALE

C HARMONIC MINOR SCALE

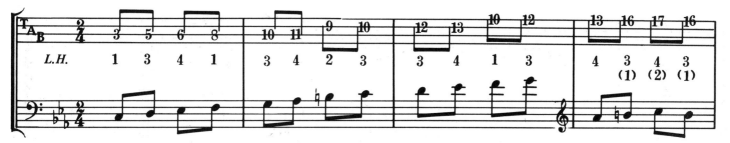

F HARMONIC MINOR SCALE

B♭ HARMONIC MINOR SCALE

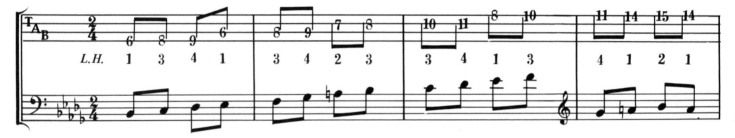

E♭ HARMONIC MINOR SCALE

Ab HARMONIC MINOR SCALE

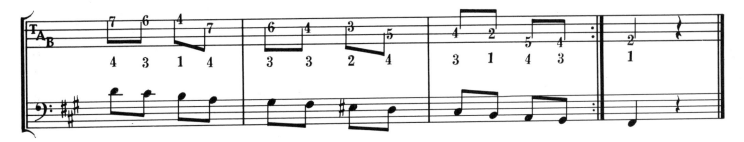

C# HARMONIC MINOR SCALE

F# HARMONIC MINOR SCALE

B HARMONIC MINOR SCALE

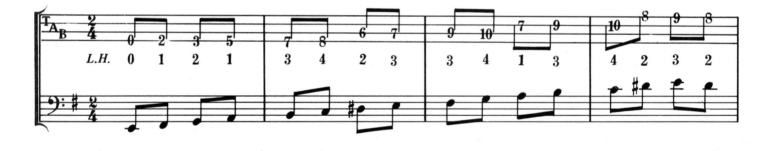

The pattern for the E harmonic minor scale is used only once because of the open 4th string.

E HARMONIC MINOR SCALE

The Melodic Minor Scales

The two octave G melodic minor scale establishes the pattern for the melodic minor scales starting on the 4th string. The position of the *1st* finger of the left hand on the 4th string tells you the letter name of the scale.

G MELODIC MINOR SCALE

The two octave C melodic minor scale establishes the pattern for the melodic minor scales starting on the 3rd string. The position of the *1st* finger of the left hand on the 3rd string determines the letter name of the scale.

C MELODIC MINOR SCALE

The two melodic minor scale patterns alternate through the cycle of fifths to complete the melodic minor scale repertoire.

A MELODIC MINOR SCALE

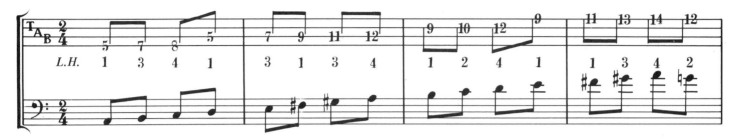

D MELODIC MINOR SCALE

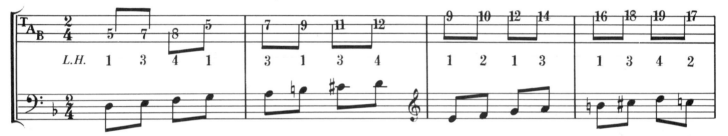

G MELODIC MINOR SCALE

C MELODIC MINOR SCALE

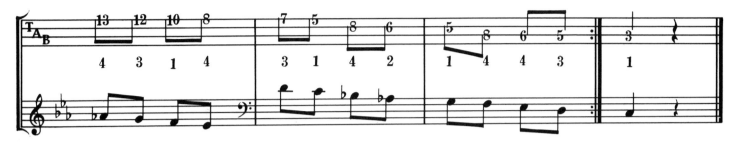

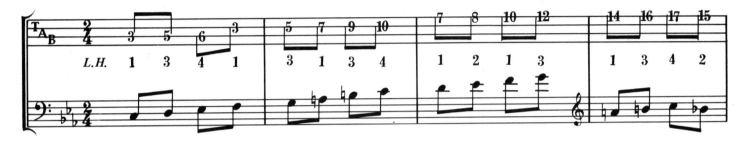

F MELODIC MINOR SCALE

Bb MELODIC MINOR SCALE

E♭ MELODIC MINOR SCALE

A♭ MELODIC MINOR SCALE

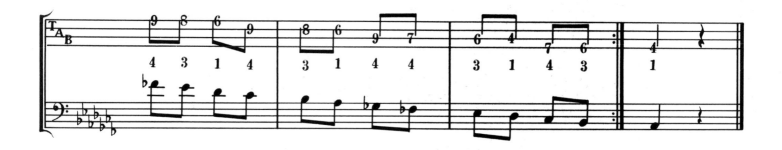

C♯ MELODIC MINOR SCALE

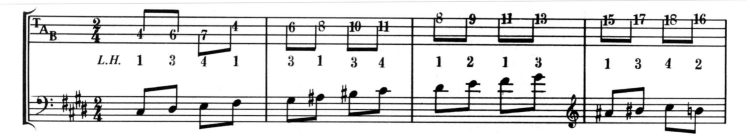

F# MELODIC MINOR SCALE

B MELODIC MINOR SCALE

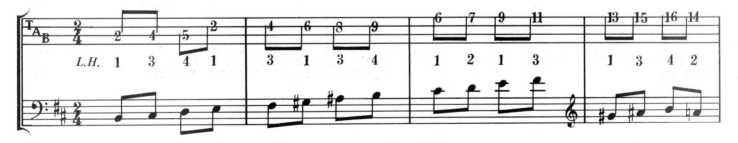

The pattern for the E melodic minor scale is used only once because of the open 4th string.

E MELODIC MINOR SCALE

The Chromatic Scale

There's really only one chromatic scale since every possible starting note is contained within it. The scale provides an excellent left hand workout.

THE CHROMATIC SCALE

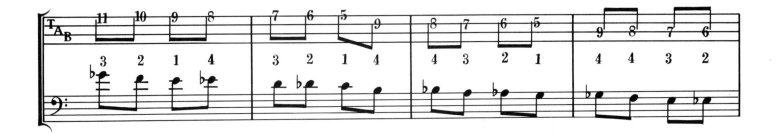

Here are some other books you might enjoy.

HARMONICS FOR ELECTRIC BASS

Here is a book that can totally revolutionize your playing. Harmonic overtones open up new worlds of expression on the bass. A special feature is the inclusion of the first-ever chord book for bass harmonics, with over 750 chords.
By Adam Novick

Order No. AM33473
U.S. ISBN: 0.8256.2267.0
U.K. ISBN: 0.7119.0335.2
$7.95/£4.95

THUMB BASICS ON ELECTRIC BASS

This book is for those who have played electric bass for some time and would like to learn "thumb technique," specifically when playing funk. Simple-to-follow text backed up with clear demonstration photos and a 10-minute soundsheet will show you exactly what to do.
By Jonas Hellborg

Order No. AM36765
ISBN: 0.7119.0503.7
$6.95/£4.50

ROCK RIFFS FOR BASS

Riffs and patterns in the styles of Jerry Jemmott, Chuck Rainey, and others. Indispensible for the bassist who needs a repertory of authentic rock styles and phrases.
By Tom Wolk

Order No. AM23508
ISBN: 0.8256.2206.9
$4.95/£3.95

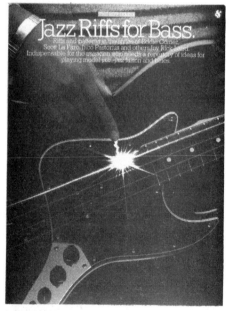

JAZZ RIFFS FOR BASS

Riffs and patterns in the styles of Jaco Pastorius, Eddie Gomez, and others. Indispensible for the bassist who needs a repertory of authentic jazz styles and phrases.
By Rick Laird

Order No. AM24605
ISBN: 0.8256.2205.0
$4.95/£2.95